Big-City School Reforms

Big-City
School
Reforms

Lessons from
New York, Toronto, and London

MICHAEL FULLAN
ALAN BOYLE

Teachers College
Columbia University
New York and London

Toronto, Ontario
Canada
www.principals.ca

Published simultaneously by Teachers College Press, 1234 Amsterdam Avenue, New York, NY 10027, and by the Ontario Principals' Council, 180 Dundas St. W, 25th Floor, Toronto, ON M5G 1Z8, Canada

Library of Congress Cataloging-in-Publication Data

Fullan, Michael.
  Big-city school reforms : lessons from New York, Toronto, and London / Michael Fullan, Alan Boyle.
       pages cm.
  Includes bibliographical references and index.
  ISBN 978-0-8077-5518-1 (pbk. : alk. paper)
  ISBN 978-0-8077-5519-8 (hardcover : alk. paper)
  ISBN 978-0-8077-7276-8 (ebook)
    1. Education, Urban—Case studies. 2. Educational change—Case studies. 3. Educational innovations—Case studies. I. Title.
  LC5115.F88 2014
  370.9173'2—dc23   2013044281

ISBN 978-0-8077-5518-1 (paper)
ISBN 978-0-8077-5519-8 (hardcover)
eISBN 978-0-8077-7276-8

Printed on acid-free paper
Manufactured in the United States of America

21 20 19 18 17 16 15 14   8 7 6 5 4 3 2 1

To urban dwellers large and small,
may they all find a learning place
and may a learning place find them

Contents

Preface

The original impetus for this book came from a group in New York City (NYC) in 2012 that came to us and said, "We have an election for a new mayor of New York City coming up on November 5, 2013. We have a notion that the tumultuous strategies used over the past decade in NYC led by Mayor Bloomberg and Chancellor Klein have been disruptive but not successful. We see that Ontario and perhaps Toronto have had a successful decade. Could you study the two situations and offer advice to the incumbent mayor for the next decade of reform?" Well, that is not the literal assignment we accepted. We did want to take a close look at big-city school reform to see what can be learned. In addition to New York City and Toronto, we examined London because of some of its successes and our personal involvement in that city's situation. Alas, the book will not be released until after the election in NYC, but it will be available as the new mayor, Bill de Blasio, and his team begin to formulate how to improve New York City schools in January 2014 and beyond. We will be interested in joining others in offering advice to those leading the next phase of reform in New York City and in other cities around the world. In other words, this book is not an empty research exercise. One other note: The three cities we are comparing are of course Western. Other revealing work is emerging from Asia—Shanghai, for example—but that will have to wait for next time.

The history of big-city system reform in education that focuses on implementation is quite recent. It was only as recently as 1988 when the first examples of districtwide reform using deliberate strategies were initiated. District 2 in New York City, with superintendent Tony Alvarado and researchers Richard Elmore and Deanna Burney, became famous for its focus on instruction and its systematic improvement in literacy and math. In Toronto, 1988 was the year the Learning Consortium began—a partnership between the University of Toronto and four large districts devoted to school and district-wide success. During that same year, 1988, Margaret Thatcher established the Education Reform Act in England, which began a wave of reforms that put Local Education Authorities (school districts) on a new path of reform. None of these efforts came from a single source. They seem to have occurred spontaneously and independently from one other. But these were early examples of big-city school reform, and when one considers the full array of local districts, such efforts remained very much in the minority during the 1990s.

As results continued to show little improvement on a wide scale, especially in reducing the achievement gaps between groups of students, the pressure for more widespread system reform mounted. A number of forces began to emerge in the late 1990s that resulted in another system reform surge, this time with whole-country and province- or state-level systems involved. England started it in 1997 when Tony Blair and Michael Barber developed a deliberate strategy for improving literacy and numeracy across England's 20,000+ primary (elementary) schools. School reform was in the spotlight once again in January 2002 when George W. Bush signed the bipartisan No Child Left Behind Act. That same year Mayor Michael Bloomberg took over New York City schools with a promise of wide-ranging reforms. Big, tough, focused new reforms began in England in Hackney and beyond, including the powerful London Challenge. In 2003 Dalton McGuinty was elected Premier in Ontario with a mandate to systematically improve the province's public school system.

The Programme for International Student Assessment (PISA) of the Organization for Economic Co-operation and Development began quietly, with its first results appearing in 2000. PISA received little attention in North America until about 2006, when the cumulative results of system work around the world attracted intensive attention, sparking interest in the reforms of Finland, Singapore, South Korea, and more recently Shanghai.

We have, then, two big pushes for system reform. The first one, spanning 1988–2001 (such cutoff points are always a bit arbitrary), remained at the district level in most jurisdictions (except for England). The second surge, during 2002–2012, brought into play big-city systems in the context of national, indeed global, reform efforts. It is this second surge that we examine in this book. We wanted to capture the reform stories of three big-city systems—New York City, Toronto, and London. Our first goal is essentially to furnish a narrative of the main elements of each story. Each one is inevitably complex, as is revealed in our case stories covered in Chapters 2 through 4.

One danger is that complex details can conceal the overall picture of what works and what does not. From our analysis of the three cases, we developed a simple framework of factors that assist big-city reform. We applied the notion of *simplexity*—to find a small number of key factors that must be at the core of the strategy (the simple part), and the chemistry of having these factors cohere in practice day after day (the complex part).[1] We also set out to focus on policy and strategy so that lessons could be derived from these efforts for other systems engaged in, or about to launch, new stages of reform. We have framed these strategies in terms of "push and pull" factors, basically concluding that all effective large-scale reform involves a judicious blend of push and pull actions. We set out the key push and pull factors in Chapter 1 and trace them through the three cases in the central chapters of the book. In Chapter 5 we derive lessons from the decade and suggest possible ways forward to achieve greater success in the future or in other cities.

This short history of district and system reform—barely 25 years old—has generated a strong knowledge base about the dos and don'ts of system reform. For the first time, the knowledge base needed to guide future big-city reform efforts is accessible. These ideas can guide efforts in the next decade—2014–2024—for greater success, all while producing additional insights that can add to our knowledge base of system reform. We hope that these experiences and lessons will serve to guide the next phase of reform. This would be a good time for history *not* to repeat itself in many jurisdictions. We have a good deal of knowledge and insights that can serve over the next decade to achieve big-city success on a scale never before seen.

Big-City School Reforms

CHAPTER 1

Tackling the Challenges of Urban Education

The heart of this book is a set of case stories of systemwide school change in three large cities: New York City, Toronto, and London. To set a broader context for those cases, in this chapter we discuss some challenges in urban education, offer a framework for tackling those challenges, and provide an overview of the national educational systems through which the case cities engaged in reform. In so doing we move from demographics to strategy and context.

In 2008, for the first time in human history, more than half of the world population lived in cities.[1] The success of urban school systems is therefore of increasing importance everywhere in the world. Urban education is both highly local and deeply national or international in nature. Much of what happens in schools, whether urban or rural, is shaped by the specifics of each place—its history, demography, political processes, and culture, as these evolve over the years. At the same time, education policy and practice are influenced to a great extent by broader economic, political, and social forces. The state of the economy influences what governments are able or prepared to do. Available technologies can affect political as well as educational decisions—witness the impact of the Internet on a variety of educational and social issues. While material conditions are important, so are ideas. People's ideas about the role of schools, or about desirable educational practices, matter a great deal, whether those ideas are well grounded in evidence or not. So a discussion of urban education should pay attention to both the general and the local.

While each city is unique, cities also have similar characteristics that affect the way education is carried out. For one thing, they tend to have more diverse populations than rural areas, whether socioeconomically, ethnically, linguistically, or in other ways. At the same time, cities tend to be more anonymous places, where neighbors are less likely to know one another and social cohesion can be weaker. People also come and go, either to and from the city or between neighborhoods, creating a more transient population. Although crime rates have fallen over the past 2 decades, cities tend to have more crime, or at least more visible crime. Street gangs are a problem in all the cities featured in this book, and one that has a significant influence on schools. And while cities are attractive places for young people such as teachers to live, they also tend to be expensive, which can make it hard to recruit and retain teachers. On a broader level, the increasing diversity in the population in each city is not only an educational challenge, but it also makes urban politics more contentious and governance more difficult. As will be evident in these cases, political and governance issues have a major impact on the ability of urban education systems to work effectively.

Yet while cities face challenges, they also have advantages when it comes to supporting good educational outcomes. They tend to be richer than rural areas, so they have more resources to put into schools. Cities have more cultural assets, such as museums and social services, with which to support schooling and children's development. Cities are also usually more tolerant of diversity in students and families. They offer the possibility of a vibrant social life and more opportunities to meet different kinds of people and explore new pathways. They generally have more employment opportunities and less-rigid social structures. All of this makes cities attractive to newcomers. Better public transit systems make many of these benefits available to more people.

A further critical contextual component to the discussion in this book is the increasing expectations for public education all around the world. It is worth remembering how recent this change is. In the 1950s it was accepted everywhere that only a small elite would succeed at university or even high school. It was broadly accepted that many, if not most, young people would get some limited schooling and then work in jobs that only demanded low levels of education. These expectations were strongly related to students' backgrounds. Now much more is expected, for many more students. Overall levels of achievement that were considered quite good 50 years ago are entirely unacceptable today. Goals that would have been thought ambitious a generation ago—for example, that virtually all students should complete secondary education—are now seen as not ambitious enough. In a way, education systems are victims of their own success, with higher levels of achievement leading to demands for still higher performance. However, this increasing success is also something to be proud of, since clearly today many people who would earlier have failed to obtain an adequate education are able to do so. And one implication of this success is to show how much people's ability to succeed in and benefit from formal education has been underestimated.

Ideas about equity in education have also changed over time. Just as expectations for the population as a whole have increased, it is no longer acceptable to assume that students will fail just because of their ethnicity, language, or family background. Higher achievement overall also draws more attention to achievement differences among population groups and efforts to make sure that all groups benefit from schooling. Increasing eq-uity in school outcomes has become a major theme in international educa-tion policy work.[2] The new mantra in education policy involves excellence and equity, a very large shift in thinking from times past.

DEMOGRAPHIC CHALLENGES FOR URBAN SCHOOL SYSTEMS

In attempting to reach the goals of excellence and equity in education, the cities we examine in this book, and many others, face two main kinds of demographic challenges—those around economic inequality and those around ethnic and linguistic diversity.

Economic Inequality Among Students

In cities, as in other settings, the most powerful single influence on student outcomes, in virtually every study, is socioeconomic status (SES). Socioeconomic status has been measured in a variety of ways. Family in-come remains the most common measure, but it has long been recognized that low income is not the only measure of hardship faced by individuals and families, and is not necessarily the best predictor of poor outcomes. In its influential PISA studies, the Organization for Economic Co-operation and Development (OECD) used measures of what might be called wealth, or "cultural capital," including the presence of certain material posses-sions in the home, such as books of poetry, dictionaries, an Internet con-nection, and the number of televisions or cars in the household, as a better measure than family income.[3]

Regardless of the measure, the environment in which children grow up has a strong effect on their life chances in every respect, including school. On average, students from less-advantaged households or families will have lower levels of achievement and poorer outcomes, while lower levels of achievement are also correlated with poorer life chances, creating a vicious circle.

While SES has a strong effect in every setting, the strength of the re-lationship appears to vary considerably across countries. PISA data show that in some countries these relationships are much stronger than in others:

- High in the United States and England
- Lower (though still significant) in Canada, the Nordic countries, and South Korea

Also, as shown in research by Wilkinson and Pickett, past a certain basic level it is not the actual level of wealth that matters in a country, but the degree of inequality. Countries with less income inequality tend to have better outcomes, not only in schooling, but in all areas of social policy.[4] Unfortunately, income inequality is rising in many countries, including the three discussed in this book, and inequality in wealth (the total value of assets) is increasing even more quickly, so the problems facing the schools in relation to socioeconomic influences on students are getting worse, not better.

International evidence shows that poverty levels are amenable to government support in areas such as income, housing, child care, and so forth.[5] Inequality has worsened in recent years, in part because of reductions in such social programs. The main policies that reduce inequality are transfer payments such as pensions, child benefits and unemployment insurance, and reasonable wage rates. Wages are especially important because poverty is not primarily the result of unemployment; most poor families have at least one full-time, year-round wage earner. However, unemployment levels are also important predictors of economic hardship.

In the face of worsening social conditions for many children, just keeping levels of achievement from declining is an accomplishment.[6] It could indeed be argued that inequalities in educational achievements are generally smaller than overall inequalities in society, suggesting that school systems have some positive effect on equality of outcomes.

Ethnic and Linguistic Diversity Among Students

While socioeconomic status is the most powerful single influence on educational outcomes, it is not the only important factor. Students' first language, ethnicity, and migration status are also important. Schools have been challenged to educate students whose cultural, linguistic, and racial characteristics differ from those of their teachers and the dominant social groups.

The connection between population diversity, poverty, and school success is more complex than the connection between poverty and school success. But there are clear patterns of failure for some groups of students, while other minority groups have very high levels of success. These factors are also often connected to socioeconomic status. Migrants and some minority groups tend to be poorer and have lower educational levels. People speaking languages other than the dominant one are often migrants and may have lower levels of education and lower incomes, in part due to discrimination in the labor market. So the various elements of disadvantage can reinforce one another. The reasons why some minorities are more successful than others are a matter of considerable dispute.

Though not taken up explicitly in this book, disability is another very strong predictor of unequal outcomes. In every system, students with disabilities of various kinds tend to lag far behind other students.

Implications for Education

Whatever the demographic indicator, it is important to keep in mind that variation in student outcomes is almost always larger within groups than between groups. In other words, there is a great deal of variation in achievement among students with the same background, and there is more variation among students of a certain ethnic background than there is between one ethnic group and another. The same applies to gender or socioeconomic status; the variation within any such group is greater than the average variation between one group and another. This is an important regularity that is often ignored in policymaking, where our attention is drawn to differences between groups. In school systems, student outcomes almost always vary more within the same class than between one class and another, and usually vary more within a school than between one school and another.

Another way of putting this relationship is to say that although poverty remains a powerful predictor of all life outcomes, it is by no means an absolute determinant. Growing up poor increases the chance of negative life circumstances, but a large proportion of children who grow up in poverty are able to construct successful lives for themselves. Indeed, a significant amount of literature shows that predictions about students' futures based on their family status are very frequently wrong and can be dangerous if they result in lower expectations.[7]

Social scientists have been interested in what factors might account for these variable outcomes, and much research has emerged in social psychology around "resilience"—the capacity of individuals to overcome highly adverse circumstances—and in sociology around "social capital"— the networks that allow communities to work together to respond productively to the challenges that they face.[8] Schools can promote resilience and social capital; they can also change the teaching and learning conditions in classrooms to be more effective with low-income students. PISA data show that countries vary significantly in their ability to support resilience among high-needs students.

Just how do these demographic factors have these effects? Micro analyses show the ways in which poverty and diversity complicate the work of schools.[9] Children and their families who live in poverty and do not share the dominant culture and language may come to school with fewer of the skills, behaviors, or understandings that teachers expect. They may have more health problems and less access to material supports such as books or study space. They are more likely to move and thus change schools more often. Their parents may be less able to help them or to advocate effectively on their behalf.

Poverty and diversity also affect how schools, teachers, and administrators do their work. Teachers may hold lower expectations for students' achievement and offer less-challenging instruction. They may struggle to provide learning experiences that engage their students and stream students into separate and segregated groups in order to teach them more easily. Timetables and curriculum may change to respond to the perceived needs and destinations of students. The time spent on behavioral management, counseling, and community liaison may increase, while instructional time decreases. None of this happens in all schools or families; the data, however, make it clear that all of these processes take place to some extent, with the result that schools are less effective at educating students who come from poor and ethnically diverse backgrounds.

Disadvantage operates cumulatively as well. For example, a child who has to move often may fall behind in schooling, even if he or she works hard and has parental support. Poor living conditions can lead to worse health, leading to more missed days of schooling. Students may then be placed in less-demanding programs with lower expectations, leading to lower performance, even while the same issues of mobility or health continue to make it more difficult for them to catch up. Parents are less able to advocate effectively for their children. One disadvantage builds on and increases the effect of another.

In some systems, it matters a great deal which school a student attends, because school quality varies greatly, or because students are streamed into particular schools based on perceived ability. In other systems, most of the variation in student outcomes is within schools; different individuals or classes have very different outcomes even within the same school. These situations have different implications for the systems. If there are large differences among schools, it is important to understand why this is so. Whatever the case may be, in order to raise achievement levels across an entire system, attention must be placed on all classrooms and on all schools, not just those with the lowest performance levels, though the latter may require higher levels of support.

ATTITUDES TOWARD EQUITY ISSUES

There is considerable disagreement about the causes of disadvantage and inequality, primarily around the degree to which these issues are seen as the result of larger social forces (among those with more liberal political views) or are seen as the result of poor individual choices (those with more conservative views). Where one stands on these questions is important because ideas about the causes of inequality are closely related to the kinds of policies that people will support. Proposals reflect the views of their proponents as to causes of poverty, so they range from efforts to get individuals to change their behavior, to proposed changes in social policy or taxation or benefit programs, to the view that poverty can only be reduced by fundamentally changing economic relations in the society.

These ideas change over time. In the 1960s there was more confidence that inequality could and should be alleviated or overcome through government action. Governments in many countries took steps to try to reduce poverty rates. That optimistic sense waned after the 1970s, but in recent years there have been active efforts in many countries to reduce discrimination and inequality in other areas, such as gender, sexual orientation, or disability.

Different arguments are also being made today around equity issues, and are focused more on the requirements of successful modern economies and societies and driven by concern about international economic competitiveness. Ideas about the importance of human capital for economic competitiveness have also been changing, with growing recognition that inequality is linked to reduced social cohesion, which is linked in turn to poorer economic growth and less attractiveness to investors.[10]

There is also growing international interest in globalization, as migration increases and countries look for new ways to reach minority and immigrant populations. Many countries are coping for the first time with the challenge of significant populations who do not speak the national language, while other countries that have long had immigrant populations are showing much greater interest in enhancing their educational success.[11]

The issues that the OECD studies often serve as a barometer of changing interests in the international education policy world. In 1996 the OECD published *Lifelong Learning for All*, a sophisticated statement about the importance of improved educational outcomes and of greater equity in those outcomes.[12] The analysis of the results of PISA has also given prominence to equity, with countries being assessed as much on the size of their achievement gap as on their overall standing.[13] In several countries the equity gaps identified in PISA have led to a fundamental rethinking of education policies. One contribution is the OECD report *No More Failures: Ten Steps to Equity in Education* (2007) and its more recent follow-up, *Equity and Quality in Education: Supporting Disadvantaged Students and Schools* (2012), the latest in a succession of OECD analyses around how to improve education outcomes broadly.

Although research plays a role in shaping these ideas, it is not often the most influential. O'Connor's conclusion about the impact of poverty research in the United States also applies to other countries:

> However impressive its data or sophisticated its models, poverty knowledge has proved unable to provide an analysis or, equally important, a convincing narrative to counter the powerful, albeit simplistic story of welfare state failure and moral decline—a narrative that, with the help of well-organized conservative analysts, has come to inform policy discourse.[14]

In a fascinating discussion of research and intellectual history, O'Connor goes on to discuss the ways in which the research enterprise itself may have contributed to poor policy choices by its reluctance to address more fundamental issues of social class, inequality, race, and gender.

STRATEGIES FOR IMPROVEMENT: BALANCING PUSH AND PULL ACTIONS

The latest efforts around the world to improve equity of outcomes from education are important, but their effectiveness depends on appropriate implementation. Talking about an achievement gap is not the same as actually doing something to reduce that gap. Inequities have remained stubbornly resistant to previous educational efforts, in large part because inequity is produced in society as a whole, not only in schools.[15]

Also, efforts to tackle inequities have been sporadic, compared with the rhetoric, and limited in the range of strategies used. If one considers the possible options—ranging from support services in schools, to early childhood development, to changed instructional practice, to community outreach, to community economic and political development—the history of the last 35 years or so shows only quite limited efforts in many domains, with little evaluation of impact.[16]

In our own work, we are not just interested in policy, but also in *strategies* employed to bring about success in big-city systems. Policies tend to be high on aspirations but skimpy on strategies. A reading of the literature on urban education gives many instances of specific programs or policy levers, but only a few instances of a coherent and systematic approach that is implemented steadily over a period of years. Payne's analysis stresses the incoherence and inconsistency of change efforts, which seem in many systems to go in different directions every few years.[17]

The lack of a systematic approach is found, though in different ways, in all three countries discussed in this book. In the United States many districts and states adopt and toss aside new education models with great regularity—typically due to the appointment of a new superintendent or the election of a new state or local leader. In such an environment, especially when coupled with the challenges already facing urban schools, real improvement seems unlikely.

In England, also, the last few years have seen many changes in policy. The Labour government issued scores of policy proposals on direction for schools between 1999 and 2010, while the current Coalition government has proposed so many changes in so many areas in just 3 years that English school leaders can hardly keep up with the proposals, let alone implement them.

By contrast, in Canada there has been much less dashing from one policy to another, but rather the opposite has occurred: very little sustained attention to issues of improving urban education. This is partly because Canada has no national system of education and no national education policy. Whereas England and the United States have suffered from too many changes, Canadian schools have seen relatively few significant reforms.

In addition to instability, effective change in education suffers from insufficient attention to implementation. As educators have known for at least 40 years, changing a complex organization requires consistent, sustained effort over time and at multiple levels.[18] The reliance on instruments such as changes in governance or accountability is inconsistent with what is known about making lasting changes in human behavior in large, complex organizations. Of course effective implementation of bad ideas is not helpful, but no change project will be effective without sustained effort, which is too often lacking in education.

Within the overall body of research, policy, and practice on system reform, we personally have been engaged in formulating, applying, and learning from reform efforts relative to what we call "whole-system change." Our own way of learning is to get in there in partnership with school and system leaders. We believe that practice produces theory better than the other way around. We use existing knowledge to inform our efforts, and then in turn learn from each effort to do it better the next time. The goal is to get a fine-grained feel for the process of dynamic change. We are also fans of *simplexity,* or what we have called "the skinny of change"; in other words, to put it a bit facetiously, we don't want any model that is as complex as the situation! No one would understand it or be able to use it. We want instead to identify the smallest number of powerful factors that when combined have a great chance of making a significant difference.

The foundational purpose of whole-system change is best expressed as "the moral imperative realized." This means having a deep commitment to raising the bar and closing the gap for *all children.* It means measuring your success in terms of what you actually accomplish by way of results. Progress must be evident for all subgroups, especially those who are disadvantaged. Because most systems are strong on aspirations and weak on concrete strategies, we focus on how partnership with others—teachers, principals, and parents—can produce actual results. Essentially, the aim of reform must include mobilizing the capacity and ownership of implementers devoted to putting effective practices into action. The reform aspirations and corresponding strategies must end up cultivating the intrinsic motivation and ability of people to put in the energy to get the results desired.

One helpful way we have used to frame the approach to whole-system change is to position what we have called "the right and wrong drivers" for reform.[19] *Drivers* are policies and associated strategies that are designed and intended to get results across the system. Wrong drivers fail to do this, while right drivers by definition are those policies that do get results. It is not that wrong drivers should be excluded, but rather that they need to be integrated in the service of the right drivers.

Currently, we are moving to more targeted sets of action-oriented change strategies that are powerful enough to dent the universe of big-system change. One of these sets of new strategies that seems promising to us concerns the concepts of *push* and *pull.* These are not original concepts, as various versions have been around for a while, including our own "pressure and support." But they are taking on a new, grounded meaning, as shown in the three cases in this book. Recently, Andy Hargreaves and one of us (Fullan) surfaced the push and pull thinking in our book, *Professional Capital.*[20] Actions that *push* are insistent, relentless, in your face, nonnegotiable. Change would not happen on a significant scale if there were no leaders who strongly challenged the status quo. But if that were all you needed, change would be easy. The problem is that "being right" is not a strategy, not to mention that you will be more wrong than right if you are only pushy. Actions that *pull* are intended to attract people to a process or situation, and to listen and learn from them as well as influence them. Pull actions can be resisted, but when they are used well, they are seductive because they tap into the twin human conditions of intrinsic motivation and social participation. By themselves, however, they are not sufficient: Just because you are attractive doesn't mean everyone will want to dance with you! People have other reasons for sitting this one out.

We hope that you are getting the picture that all successful system reform *is* a judicious mixture of push and pull actions. What *judicious* means in a given situation begs the question of what to do. If you are primarily a pushy leader, you will think that your actions are judicious; same for the pullers of the world. This is why we always link strategies to evidence of outcomes. Any lessons must stand up to the evidence; the efficacy of push–pull balance is found in the proof of the pudding: Does it work in the situation you are in? If you only push, you will either knock people over or they will push back, creating a true "gunslingers" standoff whereby while you are shooting someone, another person is shooting you. Few factors are purely push or pull, but most have central tendencies one way or the other. And finally, the model of change we offer here fits big systems that have urgent problems. There are other models that may be appropriate for other circumstances.

One of the recent formulations that we find helpful comes from Lyle Kirtman, who worked with over 600 education leaders and identified seven critical competencies.[21] We give credence to his conclusions over others because they come directly from practice. Although we are not going to use all of his competencies, we will draw on them as they map onto our cases and our identification of push and pull factors. These are Kirtman's seven competencies:

1. Challenge the status quo.
2. Build trust through communication and expectations.
3. Create a commonly owned plan for success.
4. Focus on team over self.
5. Have a high sense of urgency for change and sustainable results.
6. Commit to improvement of self.
7. Build external networks and partnerships.

In the sections below we discuss six purposeful actions—sets of three push and three pull strategies that combine to achieve results. These include some of Kirtman's competencies listed above, but we adapt those to fit into the dynamic framework we are creating, and add others to complete a balanced framework that will sustain reform efforts in big-city education systems. The "push" actions we have selected are: (1) challenge the status quo, (2) convey a high sense of urgency (with data), and (3) have the courage to intervene. The corresponding "pull" actions are: (1) create a commonly owned strategy, (2) develop professional power of capital, and (3) attend to sustainability. We see them as our version of "the skinny of big-city reform" (see Figure 1.1). It is important to note at the outset that this is not an intrinsically top-down model, although we are applying these concepts to big systems and their leaders. Teacher leaders, coaches, principals—in other words, peers—can and should employ push and pull actions. Peers can challenge the status quo, help build common strategies, build professional power, and otherwise foster changes in the culture of the system. In other words, people can push and pull upward as much as downward; and they can push and pull laterally with peers.

Figure 1.1. A Dynamic Framework of Purposeful Actions That Support Big-City Reform

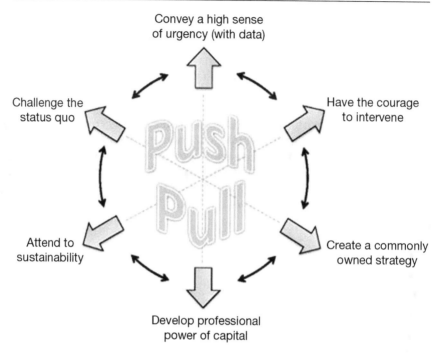

Convey a high sense
of urgency (with data)

Challenge the
status quo

Have the courage
to intervene

Attend to
sustainability

Create a commonly
owned strategy

Develop professional
power of capital

Set 1: Challenge the Status Quo/
Create a Commonly Owned Strategy

First, we consider the actions that initiate reform: challenge the status quo and then create a commonly owned strategy. Big cities have desperately urgent problems. The lives of tens of thousands of children, their parents, and future generations are at stake. Add inertia, worn ways of working, and cultures stuck continuing to do what has always been done. In such circumstances you need a powerful force or combination of forces to convey the message that under no circumstances can the status quo remain. Leaders in such situations put resources—financial and political— to back up an initiative. They create the impression that they are not going away. They don't just have aspirations; they act powerfully to cause things to happen. They are unapologetically persistent. And in all these cases there are some *nonnegotiables*—things that must be attended to, such as clear data on each and every student. So, especially when it comes to big cities, we are going to conclude that challenging the status quo is a necessary (but insufficient) condition for reform.

Here is where impatient leaders get into trouble. The goal is to commence a process of ownership-building that generates commitment through purposeful action. As David M. Cote, Chairman and CEO of Honeywell, so insightfully advised: "Your job as a leader is to be right at the end of the meeting, not at the beginning" (*New York Times*, November 3, 2013, Sunday Business, p. 2). Ownership and buy-in is a process of creating mutual meaning, clarity, and commitment for subsequent action. A successful leader needs to accompany the mandate for reform with a process that begins to build commitment and ownership to both the vision and the strategy to mobilize action. This is very hard to do because at its core this involves building trust where trust previously did not exist. Following Lyle Kirtman, we call it "creating a commonly owned strategy." It is extremely difficult to combine challenging the status quo and getting people on board and committed to a new shared plan, as many will feel threatened by the prospects of fundamental change. This is the hard work of initial implementation. There is a natural tension in this first set of strategies. The more committed leaders are to challenging the status quo, the less patient they are with developing a large constituency of implementers, who typically are a combination of some true believers, those who are unsure or unclear, and those who are opposed. We believe that some challengers of the status quo underestimate the percentage of those "out there" who are, or could be, kindred spirits—those who are also dissatisfied with the status quo. These leaders thus fail to cultivate the broad constituency that is necessary for recruiting others.

The task here is to engage in two-way communication about the new vision, high expectations, and clear strategy for getting there. It's also about staying positive and avoiding blame by focusing on issues and solutions rather than on people's weaknesses. Good leaders have initial clarity, but they refine it in interaction with others. It is a trust-building proposition that involves clarity, integrity, and competence—you have to know what you are doing and realize that developing trust will take time. When you combine the first two actions—challenging the status quo and developing a common vision—you can move fairly quickly. People admire, and give leeway to, tough-acting leaders if they operate in an open, trustworthy fashion. People do not particularly like slow-paced indecisive consensus-builders who take a long time to get to any action. Nor do they take to impositional leaders who serve the solution on a platter of policy diktat.

So the first set of recommendations is that successful leaders must balance and integrate what turns out to be a very tricky pair of push and pull forces. Their moral imperative is "children first," but only if accompanied by an adult. They know it is going to take the whole village and they set out to constantly cultivate and expand the constituency for the mission at hand. They then use the other change levers to support and drive this cause.

Set 2: Convey a High Sense of Urgency (with Data)/ Develop Professional Power of Capital

The second set combines an ongoing high sense of urgency (using data) with the development of what we call "professional power of capital." By this term we mean gathering all available resources and using them purposefully to gain the most impact. As well as material and community resources, it includes professional abilities and the mental characteristics of confidence, determination, and competition. Challenging the status quo sets the context for urgency, but leaders need to reinforce it by constantly and precisely knowing how each and every student is doing. Ongoing urgency has little credibility if it remains at the level of rhetoric. This set of factors combines the push of transparent data with the pull of using it as a strategy for improvement. To do well, a leader has to know specifically how well the system is performing. Successful systems develop strong databases that are specific to the student and all subgroups, easily and transparently accessible, and used to maintain a sense of ongoing focus and urgency. Although we call this a push factor, it is not the "hit-them-over-the-head" variety. It keeps the pressure on as it marks progress or lack therein. It is also important to use multiple measures and not just rely on a single set, such as test scores.

On the pull side of this equation, data are used as part and parcel of instructional improvement and building the professional capacity and power of the group. The result is deep ownership and the professional power of capital whereby scores of system members are pulling in the same direction. This capacity building, especially if it focuses on developing professional and community capital, accomplishes several critical things simultaneously: It builds commitment; it gives people skills essential for progress; and it generates confidence that progress is possible, thereby increasing the basis for further action.

In sum, balance is the key—urgent data, staring you in the face, combined with the wherewithal to use data with specificity for improvement and for celebration as the system progresses. Leaders cannot get anywhere unless they mobilize the talents and commitment of the vast majority of system members working for a common purpose using targeted data as the focus.

Set 3: Have the Courage to Intervene/Attend to Sustainability

The final set—having the courage to intervene and attending to sustainability—serves to keep momentum going while introducing fresh initiatives. Intervention occurs from the beginning, but it is largely used to build capacity in the system. The message should be that *all schools* must improve if the system is to sustain itself (stated in reverse, if some schools are not improving, it weakens the system context for reform). Thus district leaders and others are willing to intervene when necessary, even—one could say especially—when the overall system is on the move. If leaders have evidenced a balanced approach relative to the first two sets of factors, the system will let them get away with strong intervention in the case of persistently failing schools, by this time in the minority.[22] These actions must be available and represent another continuous push force.

The flip side of attending to persistent problems is to pay attention to conditions of sustainability. Some of these conditions will have been addressed in the previous two pull factors of commitment to a common vision and strategy and the development of professional power. Feeding forward to sustainability includes the following:

- The continuous attention to recruitment of leaders and other personnel
- Professional learning that deepens professional capital
- Retaining skilled people to get maximum return on your investment
- Attention to detail (such as constantly focusing on quality implementation)
- Creating an infrastructure that maintains continuous action on implementing a small number of ambitious goals
- Oddly enough, to get future sustainability you have to engage in innovation that promises a new effective order

Innovation is related to sustainability because there are always better ways of improving and adding to what is being done. Going deeper into learning, improving early learning, and using technology to develop new pedagogical–learning partnerships are some of the innovations possible.

So we believe this framework of six push and pull factors meets our *simplexity* criterion of a small number of core factors that are easy to understand, though difficult to use in combination. We do stand by our main conclusion that big-city change requires a sophisticated combination and merging of strong push and strong pull factors. Leaders need relentless drive, but they also need to fashion deep and widespread capacity, commitment, and ownership. Balance and integration of the two forces is key. We think that eventually they feed on one another. Strong pull has a push of its own as peers and other system leaders get better and demand more of themselves and one another. Strong push awakens people to the urgency of the situation, where they can become push and pull agents of their own. While the educational challenges of big cities can be horrendous, we have tried to show by examining the cases of New York City, Toronto, and London that they can be tackled successfully. In subsequent chapters we use our push–pull framework in presenting and analyzing each of the three case stories.

THE NATIONAL EDUCATIONAL CONTEXTS OF THE CASE CITIES

Understanding the education reform efforts of New York City, Toronto, and London requires some basic awareness of the differences among the national systems in which our case cities operate their schools. Without attempting to be comprehensive or definitive, we review some of the key areas of difference among the United States, Canada, and England.

Policy

Policy is most uniform in England, less so in Canada, and most variable in the United States, which due to its size, diversity, and emphasis on local control has a system in which very few things can be said to be common, let alone universal. The U.K. national government makes education policy for England (Scotland, Wales, and Northern Ireland have their own education policies). In the United States education is a responsibility of the states, but the federal government plays an influential role in shaping policy direction, providing funding in some areas and supporting research. In Canada there is no national minister or ministry of education, and the 13 provinces and territories have control over their education systems.

Governance and Finance

All three countries have local authorities for education. In England the local authorities are also responsible for other municipal services, while the other two countries have locally elected school boards that deal only with schools (with the notable exception that over the last decade in the United States more and more big-city systems, such as New York City, have boards and chancellors appointed by mayors). In England, national policy has steadily reduced the influence of local authorities so that they have very little control over individual schools. In the United States the 14,000 or so school districts (most of them with very small enrollments) still provide the bulk of funding for education in most states, and are powerful players in the system. Canada's 400 or so school districts are in between—more powerful than in England but not as much as in the United States—since Canadian provincial governments have increasingly taken control over education policy. In Canada and the United States schools' principals and teachers are employed by districts, but in England individual schools employ their own staff.

In England funding for schools comes primarily from the national government, with most of it flowing directly to individual schools via formulas and grant programs. In the United States 44% of funding still comes from local districts, 43% from states, and 13% from the federal government, though these numbers vary a lot from state to state.[23] In Canada provincial governments provide essentially all the money for schools, since the revenue-raising powers of school boards have been decreased or eliminated in most of the country in the last 20 years.

Curriculum and Assessment

Curriculum is set nationally in England, provincially in Canada, and by the state or locally in the United States, although the recent Common Core State Standards (CCSS) are bringing some nationwide elements to U.S. curriculum (it is beyond our focus to take up CCSS in detail, but essentially most states [over 90%, including New York] have signed on to a national effort to define high standards in all academic subject areas, and to develop corresponding assessment standards, which are to be ready by 2014–2015). New York State adopted the Common Core Standards in 2009–10. In 2010–11 the NYC Department of Education launched the Common Core pilots in 100 schools, with all schools scheduled to implement citywide instructional expectations by 2012. And by 2013 Common Core Standards were to be integrated into state tests for Grades 3–8.

Assessment of students occurs nationally at ages 11 and 16 in England. In the United States each state has its own assessment policy that may or may not be linked to curriculum, though there may be more common assessments as part of the introduction of the Common Core Standards. In Canada provinces have student assessment policies, with most testing students at two or three grade levels and by some high school exit exams. All of these are curriculum based. In Canada such assessments are mostly low-stakes for both students and schools, whereas in the United States the stakes are often very high for schools and sometimes for students, and in England are high both for students and schools.

Educational Organizations

England has an important set of national institutions and organizations for education, such as the National College for Teaching and Leadership (recently moved from an arm's-length agency to a government department) and the Office for Standards in Education (Ofsted). The

United States has many organizations playing some role in education, from foundations (some of which are very influential), to research and policy centers, to various lobby groups. Canada has a weak national infrastructure with few important national organizations, and correspondingly limited ongoing policy connections across provinces. Teacher unions have more influence and negotiating power in the United States and Canada (although this varies by state/province) than in England for two reasons: In England teachers are divided between several different unions, and as the local authorities no longer have direct power over individual schools, unions cannot negotiate with them on behalf of teachers.

Summary and Comparison of the Case City Education Systems

While New York City, Toronto, and London are roughly comparable in size, they each have very different education systems. We compare the three systems in Figure 1.2 using data from 2012. We should note that the Toronto District School Board, the focus of our case study, is the central board in the Greater Toronto Area (GTA) and consists of 591 schools organized into 24 families of schools with 260,000 students in Grades K–12—this is an autonomous subset of the larger GTA configuration.

CONCLUSION

In summary, the body of research on urban education points to four key conclusions that provide a context for the next three chapters.

First, the problems of urban education are multiple and extend beyond the schools, drawing our attention to the reciprocal relationship between schools and the societies in which they exist. It is much harder to provide effective education in societies that are highly unequal in other ways. Yet schools facing similar conditions can also have quite different levels of effectiveness. So, while recognizing the powerful impact of social forces, we know that schools and school systems can make an important difference.

Second, disadvantage exists and operates in multiple forms, involving socioeconomic status, ethnicity, immigration status, first language, gender, special educational needs, and other elements. The more disadvantages a student faces, the greater his or her odds of struggling in school. Yet the literature on prediction and resilience also tells us that many students are able to do well even under very difficult conditions, reinforcing the point that background is not destiny, at least not at the level of the individual.

Third, meaningful improvement will require a systemic strategy that leads to actions across multiple elements of the system in a coherent way.

Figure 1.2. Comparison of Three Big-City Education Systems: New York City, Toronto (Greater Toronto Area), and London in 2012

	New York City	Toronto (GTA)	London
Regulated by	New York State	Ontario Province	UK government
No. of public schools	1,602	1,894	1,304
No. of charter schools/ academies	123	–	139
No. of students	1,038,066	972,345	1,141,510
Funded by	City (48%) State (42%) Federal (10%)	Provincial government	UK government
Average spent per student in US$	$18,612	$10,550 (C$10,916)	$9,129 (£5,977)
City administration	Central control by NYC Department of Education (DoE), headed by a chancellor appointed by the mayor	No coordination across Greater Toronto Area	No coordination across London
Organization	32 elected Community Education Councils liaise with NYC DoE	5 district school boards (DSB) 5 Catholic DSB 2 French-language boards	32 elected local authorities procure services for schools
Decision-making	Panel for Educational Policy (PEP) appointed by mayor and five boroughs	Elected board of trustees for each DSB	Individual school governing bodies
Accountability	NYC Progress Reports combine data from state tests with teacher/ parent/student survey NYC Quality Review with clear judgments and published reports State and federal evaluations	Provincial tests School district reviews with confidential nonjudgmental reports	National tests School inspections with clear judgments and published reports

Just tackling one or two aspects is very unlikely to be enough, yet that kind of sporadic approach has been the dominant mode in most places. Strategies should be well grounded in evidence on which actions are likely to yield the greatest benefit for the least effort. This would mean a move away from approaches to education policy that are highly ideological.

Finally, dynamic implementation efforts sustained over time are vital, yet also not the norm. The complexities of changing large school systems are typically badly underestimated, leading to insufficient political, material, and psychological effort, and ultimately failure. Our framework of push and pull dynamics provides six purposeful actions that together offer a better chance of raising standards of student achievement across the system.

In the next three chapters we delve into the big-city cases one by one to see what can be learned from the reform process in each city. Our study involves the following facets:

- Providing a narrative account of the main changes in each school system between 2002–2012
- Analyzing students' standardized test scores and graduation rates over the same period
- Connecting the reforms to our dynamic framework of purposeful actions that support big-city reform (refer to Figure 1.1)
- Drawing conclusions as to what policies and strategies are most effective for big-city reform

The history of these reforms is constructed from secondary sources such as research reports, written accounts, and contemporary stories published in the news media. This is supplemented in each case with our own firsthand knowledge plus conversations with education leaders in each city. Our analysis of test scores and graduation rates is based on primary source data.[24] And our evaluation is drawn from the evidence we have collected. Our goal in this book is to understand the decade of 2002–2012 in order to draw lessons for improving the future of big-city reform. In short, we are interested in which policies and strategies generate quality implementation that in turn maximizes the benefits for students as measured by raising the bar for all, and reducing the gap for the disadvantaged.

CHAPTER 2

New York City

Restructuring over Reculturing

New York City has attracted enormous attention over the past decade for its education reform efforts for several reasons: It is a large prominent system; it represents an aggressive, relentless attempt by a mayor and his appointed chancellor to pull out all the stops to get successful reform; and it was carried out in a transparent, high-profile manner. Everyone in the school reform community was watching! The reform effort, called "Children First," was initiated by Mayor Michael Bloomberg in 2002. It is a complicated history, but well documented.

SETTING THE SCENE

With an estimated population of 8,336,697 in 2012, New York City is the largest city in the United States.[1] The city is divided into five municipal boroughs (see Figure 2.1). Unlike other urban areas in the United States, all schools in NYC are administered by one system, the NYC Department of Education, making it by far the biggest education system in the United States and one of the largest in the world.

Build Up to Reforms

In the latter part of the 1990s the number of failing schools in NYC was on the rise with no apparent strategy to attack the problem. Mayor Rudolph W. Giuliani expressed his growing frustration during his budget address in 1999: "The system is just plain terrible, it makes no sense, and the end result of it is that if this were a business system, it would be in bankruptcy." He added, "The whole system should be blown up and a new one should be put in its place."[2]

The New York City Board of Education was established by the state of New York in 1969 to buffer schools from political intervention.[3] Its seven members were appointed by the mayor and the presidents of the city's

Figure 2.1. Boroughs of New York City

five boroughs. The board's job was to appoint a school chancellor, determine policy, and ensure the successful operation of its schools. From 1970, elementary and middle schools were administered by 32 community school districts (CSDs), each with an elected board that controlled policy and appointed its own superintendent. The NYC Board of Education administered high schools across the city and support for special education and English language learners. By 2000, one-third of the CSDs were well run, one-third had a reputation for overcrowded schools or downplaying the needs of schools with mainly Black and Hispanic students, while the other third was characterized by patronage and corruption.[4] Pressure was growing to abolish the Board of Education and turn the schools over to the mayor as Boston, Chicago, Cleveland, and Detroit had done.[5] The system survived the remainder of Giuliani's term of office, but not beyond.

Any change to the administration of the NYC Board of Education needed approval by the New York State Legislature. In July 2001 Sheldon Silver, Speaker of the New York State Assembly, formed a task force to consider alternatives to the NYC Board of Education. In November 2001, Michael R. Bloomberg was elected to the office of mayor with the support of the popular outgoing Mayor Giuliani. Bloomberg is a billionaire businessman who emphasized education during his campaign. His first undertaking was to gain mayoral control of the education system.

Through February and March 2002 the New York City Council Committee on Education considered the issue. They heard testimony from witnesses during a series of five hearings. At the fifth and final hearing in March, the president of the Board of Education, Ninfa Segarra, gave the following testimony regarding the Board of Education:

> You cannot have an institution with a $12 billion budget, more importantly serving over a million children in over 1,000 schools . . . to be separate from the rest of the city's governing system. I have seen the results up close and personal for 12 years, it is a nightmare. . . .
>
> It is a bureaucracy that is accountable to no one; it is a bureaucracy that does not answer questions parents and citizens ask and it does not follow the directions they're given. It is a bureaucracy that runs roughshod over parents, community leaders, and elected officials. It is a bureaucracy that is not governed by a clear educational vision that spends money with ever-increasing energy, yet cannot measure consistent progress toward any meaningful goals. . . .
>
> To the people who say that our broken schools can be fixed if the system now in place just worked a little differently, we need to say, "No. Enough is enough! You have had your chance." We need to clear away the debris and the barriers from all the failed and futile attempts at halfway reforms of previous years. And then we can say to the Mayor, "These are our children and our schools, you are our elected leader, let's do it."[6]

Following up on Segarra's invitation, Mayor Bloomberg presented his vision for education in New York City to the same committee:

> Very simply, I seek a school system that ensures a quality education for every student, where results are not a function of student demographics, but are the product of a system that values achievement by all students.
>
> I seek a system that encourages parental participation in our diverse city; one that strengthens the work of the entire school system.
>
> I seek a system that expects students to meet high standards for educational achievement and prepares them for the challenges that an increasingly complex and competitive world presents.

I seek a system that holds managers responsible for the success or failure of individual units based upon the results that parents have a right to expect, measurable, relevant educational achievements by all our children.

I seek a system that treats teachers as professionals who are rewarded and respected for high-quality work, by providing them with the tools, the environment, and the training they need to be most effective.

I seek a system that focuses on teaching and learning for students as our primary mission, rather than, as in the past, many times just providing custodial services for some of our children.

And I seek a system that provides a totally safe environment that balances the needs of disruptive students with the equally important rights of those who want to learn.[7]

At the following meeting on March 19, eight of the nine members of the committee voted in favor of mayoral responsibility for education and one abstained.[8] This was later approved by New York State, and Mayor Bloomberg took control of the Board of Education on July 29, 2002, initially until the end of June 2009.

In 2002 Raymond Domanico wrote a report for the Center for Civic Innovation about the state of NYC public schools.[9] Having served as Director of Data Analysis for the NYC Board of Education in the 1980s, with 20 years of experience in educational research, he was well qualified to judge. His report covered the preceding 5 years; it provides a baseline from which we can measure progress over the next decade. Domanico reported that in 2002:

- Only 50% of students completed high school either with a diploma (46%) or GED (4%) within 4 years. These figures were unchanged from the 1990s.
- Only 19% of students scored 65% or more in five New York State Regents exams (which became the New York State graduation requirement in 2012).
- In elementary and middle schools, only 41% of students were proficient in reading and 34% in mathematics, according to the citywide tests in 2000.

He claimed that many areas of the city were "educational dead zones," citing seven entire districts where fewer than 30% of students passed the city English exam, and those seven plus another seven districts (14 out of 32) had less than 30% of students passing the math exam. Test scores were generally very low and stagnant. Because the Board of Education had endured a series of mishaps with its testing program at the turn of the millennium, comparison with previous years was impossible.[10] Domanico observed that the performance of the school system was not improving.

Ad Hoc Successes in the City

Although overall test scores were low in 2002, there were examples of outstanding success in NYC that had been recognized and celebrated both nationally and internationally:

- Community School District 13 in Brooklyn was characterized by a succession of outstanding superintendents. They emphasized tight centralized management, curriculum control, no-excuses accountability, and strong parental involvement.[11]
- The transformation of Community School District 4 in East Harlem during the 1980s drew international acclaim. They promoted choice through the creation of small, innovative schools with the freedom to adopt their own curriculum and instructional practices.[12]
- The development of small high schools in cities across the country was influenced by the extraordinary success of schools like Central Park East Secondary School, within the Alternative High School District.[13]
- Community School District 2 in Manhattan made remarkable gains in the 1990s through a relentless focus on instruction and professional learning. They looked outward to identify the best approaches to literacy and numeracy around the world and used them to develop balanced literacy and mathematics programs that were implemented in all schools.[14]
- The Coalition Campus Schools project replaced two failing high schools in Manhattan and the Bronx with eleven small successful high schools on shared sites in 1992. With support from the teacher unions, they were able to hire staff according to school needs rather than seniority.[15]
- The New York Networks for School Renewal project created a virtual district called the Learning Zone in 1994 that promoted systemic change through greater autonomy coupled with accountability.[16] They also piloted a New York City version of the English school inspection model.
- Just before the new administration took over in 2002, the New Century High Schools initiative set out ambitious plans to replace large failing high schools with smaller schools on a larger scale. With support from teacher unions and additional funding, New

Century invited organizations outside the system to partner in the design and development of these schools.[17]

Domanico's report conveyed a high sense of urgency backed up with reliable data and offered Mayor Bloomberg, who has never lacked courage, the right to take dramatic action. To anticipate one of our later conclusions, there are often pockets of success in large systems that to us represent the potential for more systematic reform. The strategy question is whether new leaders appreciate these ad hoc successes (which are really against the odds) in order to understand the conditions under which schools improve. Usually they do not and, in a hurry to alter the entire system, often throw out the baby with the bathwater. In any case, in 2002 there was widespread support at the central leadership level to overthrow the whole system. In our dynamic framework these are all push actions that need to be balanced by matching pulls. In the absence of the development of pull factors, one can predict that whatever new successes there might be will not be sustainable. We now examine the reforms to see to what extent they pulled people with them.

CHILDREN FIRST REFORMS

Soon after taking control of the NYC school system, Mayor Bloomberg replaced the Board of Education with a 13-member Panel for Educational Policy (PEP). Eight PEP members are appointed by the mayor, and one from each of the five boroughs is appointed by the borough president.[18] Bloomberg appointed Joel I. Klein to run the New York City school system. Klein was a former U.S. Justice Department lawyer and a surprising choice to most observers at the time.[19] Together, they immediately set about taming the system.

The strategic development of Children First reforms from 2002–2012 began with centralization and tight control followed by increasing deregulation from 2005 onward. Some commentators claim, with hindsight, that the actions to first centralize control then decentralize it were necessary in order to break down the entrenched bureaucracies within the 32 community school districts that had obstructed earlier reform efforts.[20] Others regard it as something more pragmatic in that after a few years in office Chancellor Klein became increasingly aware that tight central management would not improve schools very much.[21] Whatever the reasoning was, the two phases of reform are distinct, and we deal with them chronologically before moving on to other aspects of the reforms. After a period of overhaul, the Children First reforms were implemented beginning in September 2003.[22]

Centralization: Phase I

The first wave of reforms were about creating greater coherence through centralized control, possibly following the successes achieved earlier in Community School Districts 2 and 13, as reported above. The reorganization used a corporate model of top-down control. It created an impression that the chancellor planned to run the school system like a business. This perception was reinforced by his selection of young, Ivy League–educated noneducators to form his leadership team; they were mostly lawyers, management consultants, and business school graduates.[23] Some considered the new "educrats" a long-awaited influx of exceptional talent, while others viewed their appointment as an insult to the veteran school officials they replaced.

Briefly, the key initial features of Children First were:

- *Organizational structure.* The 32 community school districts, with community school boards, were replaced by 10 instructional divisions based on geographical regions. Each of the 10 regional superintendents managed up to 10 local instructional supervisors (LISs) who worked with about 10 schools each. This established clear lines of accountability from the chancellor to every school principal. Finance and operational management were separated from instruction and transferred to six regional operating centers.
- *Common curriculum.* Apart from 200 high-performing schools, all elementary and middle schools had to follow the same reading and mathematics programs mandated by the NYC Department of Education and based on the balanced literacy program used in former CSD 2.
- *Instruction.* Schools were assigned literacy and mathematics coaches who worked in schools but reported to the LISs. They imposed a prescribed pedagogy with detailed daily activities.
- *Principals.* They were given more control of their budgets and increased discretion over hiring their deputies.
- *Capacity building.* The creation of New York Leadership Academy, using private-sector funding, was announced. It was launched in 2003 with a mission to prepare principals for New York City's high-needs schools.
- *Parental involvement.* Each school hired a parent coordinator to do outreach and help parents engage with the system. Parental support centers were open 2 nights a week and on weekends.

In 2002 it was estimated that there were more than 70 different literacy programs in use across NYC elementary schools, with varying levels of effectiveness, and just about every mathematics program imaginable.[24] The Children First reform argued for equity by imposing what were considered to be proven, effective ways to establish children's core academic skills. Klein recruited Diana Lam, who had implemented similar reforms in San Antonio, TX, and Providence, RI, as deputy chancellor for curriculum and instruction. Lam came on a huge salary with a track record of successful system turnaround and a reputation for alienating teachers.[25]

The choice of balanced literacy and mathematics programs was logical, as they were favored by Lam and NYC already had significant leadership capacity for these instructional methods from CSD 2. Yet both are still considered to be controversial teaching methods, shunning phonics and emphasizing conceptual formation in mathematics, which critics dubbed "fuzzy math."[26] Problems emerged later when the literacy program failed to meet federal requirements for financial support under the No Child Left Behind (NCLB) program. A huge professional development program was rolled out to support 85,000 teachers. Despite that, or maybe because of it, the prescribed curriculum created a growing controversy as many teachers resented what they considered was micromanagement by the chancellor.[27] Using our framework to analyze the dynamics, there was too much push and too little pull. Responding to complaints from some successful schools, Klein allowed exemptions if they could make a good case to use alternative instructional programs based on their students' test scores. If a given policy increasingly require concessions, it is a certain sign that the policy is flawed.

Politics

In March 2004, just 6 months into the Children First reform, Bloomberg and Klein were involved in their first serious political controversies. Chancellor Klein dismissed deputy Lam on the grounds that she had used her position to fix a job for her husband in the school system without conflict-of-interest clearance. In her parting shot, Lam revealed conflict in the NYC Department of Education between longtime New York City educators and the new management experts from the private sector. As an outsider to both camps, Lam suggested that she was a scapegoat for the negative reactions to the balanced literacy program from federal authorities.[28]

A few days later Mayor Bloomberg chose to assert his authority in what was called the "Monday Night Massacre" over the end of social promotion.[29] Bloomberg had replaced the old Board of Education with the new Panel for Educational Policy and stacked it with his appointed representatives to ensure that his policies would be unhindered. When Bloomberg proposed that students at Level 1 should be held back in 3rd grade, some members of the panel objected. On the day of the vote, the mayor fired two of his appointees and ensured the departure of a third, so that his policy was approved. After the meeting he said: "Mayoral control means mayoral control, thank you very much. These are my representatives and they are going to vote for things that I believe in."[30] Described as "Politics first, children last" by parents, the mayor's action indicated his intention to dismiss opposition and kicked off growing frustration among parents and the community about their lack of influence on public education. This is a powerful example of push–pull dynamics in action. Bloomberg was completely frustrated by his own appointed representatives, and in order to enforce his will he used too much push, undermining the possibility of building support for later implementation. With hindsight, we suggest that the lack of balance here contributed to the loss of support from the community, which eventually stalled reforms in Bloomberg's third term.

Autonomy Zone

After a year in control, Klein started to loosen up the system. Twenty-nine high schools (including three charter schools) were selected to form the "Autonomy Zone" in September 2004. In exchange for increased funding, budgetary freedom, and school-based management, principals voluntarily signed 5-year contracts that specified performance targets including test scores, attendance, and graduation rates. The consequences for failing to meet these targets were clear and more aggressive than those in the federal (NCLB) or state accountability systems. If a school in the Autonomy Zone missed its targets for a 2nd year, the principal would be fired; after a 3rd year the school would be closed.[31] Schools in the zone were not required to follow any mandated curriculum, and they no longer reported to their regional superintendent. Instead, they were monitored by former principal and superintendent Eric Nadelstern, CEO of the Autonomy Zone. Nadelstern, a 35-year veteran of NYC education, was clear that the purpose of the zone was to show that giving principals and faculty the opportunity to make decisions in their students' best interests would be more likely to improve performance.[32] In our framework, this is a cautious pulling action using a small group of schools as a test bed.

In order to give all principals across the city more power to hire staff, a collective agreement with the teachers' union was negotiated in 2005 to end the process known as "seniority bumping," under which principals were forced to hire teachers by seniority if they applied for a vacancy at their school. After 2005 principals could interview all candidates and appoint the best applicant irrespective of seniority. Teachers who lost their jobs through budget cuts or school closures and were unable to get appointed to another school were offered substitute teacher positions. The union negotiated a 15% pay raise for teachers and a new position of Lead Teacher, with a $10,000 additional allowance, was created.[33] This was a landmark agreement for growing autonomy in NYC.

In the school year 2005–2006, another 19 schools joined the zone, making 48 in total. In the same year Chancellor Klein established the Office of Accountability and appointed Jim Liebman, a respected civil rights lawyer, as Chief Accountability Officer. Liebman's brief was to design and implement an accountability system. By now it seems that Klein was committed to an autonomy–accountability exchange with schools. With a robust accountability system in place, he could offer schools more autonomy and shift power from the center to the school principals.

In January 2006 Klein announced that he was planning another major reorganization of the system, seeking to cut $200 million from central and regional administrative budgets and freeing at least another 150 schools from the oversight of superintendents provided the schools met specific performance goals.[34] This was the overture of Phase 2: "What we are seeking is a system of great schools, not a great system of schools."[35] At that stage, Klein was quite pushy, making specific performance goals a condition for autonomy. Nadelstern had the opposite view, which was more inclined to pull schools along. He was convinced in 2005 that autonomy was the prerequisite for higher school performance; what they were seeking was a way to make it scalable to the entire system.[36] We will speculate here to say that many school leaders prefer collaboration over win–lose autonomy, but most will play the game and try to survive under prevailing conditions (not to mention the probability that constant structural reorganizations—and more to come as we will see—make it difficult to know what given arrangements actually mean or whether they would stay in place).

Deregulation and Empowerment: Phase 2

Mayor Bloomberg was elected for his second term in November 2005. The second phase of Children First reforms started in the 2006–2007 school year. The Autonomy Zone was renamed the Empowerment Zone, and all schools were invited to join. There was a significant shift in policy. Klein was now saying that if the system empowered principals and held them accountable for school results, it would achieve two things:

- Shift power from the central office to schools
- Change the culture of the system to focus on results

While autonomy itself did not necessarily lead to success, Klein was convinced by Nadelstern and evidence from the Autonomy Zone that it would produce more innovation at school level that the system could learn from. In the fall of 2006 the Empowerment Zone started with 332 schools (including 10 charter schools), roughly a quarter of the schools in the city. This made it the fifth largest school system—if it could be called that—in the United States.

Inviting schools to join the Empowerment Zone and creating the autonomy–accountability exchange is a good example of balanced push–pull dynamics in our framework. However, the sudden expansion was harshly criticized, especially by those who considered that autonomy should be earned by schools with proven leadership capacity, and Nadelstern was taken to task by the City Council Committee on Education in March 2007.[37] Nadelstern argued that principals, in consultation with parents and teachers, were best placed to make decisions about their own students' learning and how to make improvements. Evidence from the pilot Autonomy Zone showed that all schools in the zone improved graduation rates and reduced dropouts compared with the city averages. Schools in the zone for 2 years outperformed their 1st-year achievements. His view that autonomy was a necessary prerequisite for better performance was now the department policy, as only principals under disciplinary investigation or schools in state or federal receivership were barred from joining the Empowerment Zone.[38] Department policy was explicit that empowerment is the way to attract the best and brightest school leaders.[39]

School Support Organizations

Nadelstern's deputy, Veronica Conforme, went on to explain to the same committee that the 332 schools in the Empowerment Zone had formed 14 voluntary networks providing support, guidance, and advocacy for the schools in their network. While Nadelstern and Conforme may not have appeased their critics on the City Council Committee on Education (who could express their concerns but had no control over policy), they were describing the shape of things to come. In September 2007 the 10 geographical regions, established in 2003, were disbanded, together with the mandated curriculum for English language arts and mathematics. The administrative budget from the regional bureaucracy was devolved to schools, and the whole system was turned upside down.[40] Instead of schools being accountable to their regional instructional division, schools were allowed to choose between three types of school support organizations (SSOs) and pay them for their services from the increased school budget.

Within their selected SSO, schools were also able to choose which network of schools to join. A network included 20–25 schools, often based on existing connections between schools. Each network was able to hire a team to provide functional expertise in instruction, assessment, business operation, special education, statutory compliance, English language learners, and youth development. To support the SSOs, five integrated service centers (ISCs) were created. They advised the networks and schools on more technical issues around human resources, payroll, health, suspensions, and other compliance issues that schools face.

Structural reorganization is a favorite systemwide approach to reform (and not just in education) by new leaders who have power. For system leaders, it is within their control and they are seductively drawn to this kind of action because they feel like, and it looks like, they are doing something. Unless it has direct impact on what happens in classrooms, it is unlikely to improve students' achievement. Larry Cuban, for example, documents 40 years of structural reform in American education that has repeatedly failed to penetrate "the black box of classroom practice."[41] In the decade of reform we are examining, structural reform was repeatedly used by the NYC Department of Education to the extent that schools had barely come to terms with the last reorganization when another one was thrust on them. Top-down reorganizations are a push strategy, and unless they are accompanied by equally strong pull factors of capacity building and collaboration, they will only give change a bad name. Both time and patience seemed to be in short supply in NYC over this decade, as there was an urgent need to improve schools within the 7 years allocated for mayoral control by New York State. Unintentionally, these massive reorganizations caused confusion and sucked energy away from principals' key priorities around instructional leadership.

Accountability System

The new SSOs did not supervise the schools; all direct supervision was eliminated. Every principal was required to set 5-year targets and would be held accountable for them. Responsibility for monitoring schools was transferred to the Office of Accountability, which Klein had established in January 2006 under Jim Liebman. When designing the accountability system, Liebman claimed that it was mainly about capacity building.[42] For us, capacity building is not simply a matter of autonomy, nor is it furthered by what we call "individualistic" strategies of developing better individual leaders—you have to develop the "group" as well. Nor is capacity building helped much by the availability of "tools"—even the best ones are necessary, but not sufficient (as the saying goes, a fool with a tool is still a fool!).

To make the lever of accountability as powerful as possible, the system would provide schools with the information they needed to be self-sufficient in evaluating themselves and solving their own problems or asking for the specific help they required. Liebman's accountability system would also spread knowledge about what works from one school to another. But again we say, capacity building is not just knowing what successful schools are doing; you actually have to be helped to develop the competencies individually and as a group. We will come back to this point later because the system seemed to be designed with sophisticated capacity-building features, including three tools for schools' self-improvement. Our point will be that accountability prevailed while capacity building was sporadic.

In April 2006 Chancellor Klein announced that the accountability system had two main components.[43] Each school would be assessed using a combination of quantitative and qualitative measures:

- A Progress Report with an A, B, C, D, or F grade derived from quantitative data
- A Quality Review, or external school audit carried out by educators, with three qualitative judgments: well developed, proficient, or underdeveloped

Consequences, based on carrot-and-stick principles, were attached to the system. High-scoring schools would later be rewarded with merit pay, and schools with chronically low scores would face increasing sanctions, including leadership change and ultimately closure. Liebman's accountability system had both elements of push–pull dynamics. It was deliberately designed to develop the professional power of teachers and leaders in schools, although it did not actually function to develop widespread capacity. At the same time, it generated a high sense of urgency by focusing on reliable data about students' achievements; good balancing actions. And it was tough on accountability to reassure a rightly skeptical community.

At the start of Phase 2 in fall 2006, the accountability system was only partially developed and it evolved, like school autonomy, over the following years.

Progress Reports. Initially, Progress Reports combined three separate quantitative measures that were weighted to generate the letter grade:

- Students' progress (55%)—tracked the progress made by individual students from one year to the next according to scores in English language arts (ELA) and mathematics in state tests
- Students' performance (30%)—reported average student performance on state tests or Regents examinations
- School environment (15%)—combined attendance data (5%) with the results of a Learning Environment user survey (10%) that

collected teachers', parents', and students' (Grades 6–12) opinions about each school and its principal

The Progress Report has evolved since 2007.[44] Further sophistications were made by comparing each school with its peer group in terms of student demographics. While the outcomes are headlined as a single letter grade, the detailed analysis within each report provides valuable information for school leaders and is available to all parents on the NYC Department of Education website (schools.nyc.gov/Accountability/tools/report/default.htm).

Quality Review. While the Progress Report is based mainly on student test scores, it is always a historic measure of past performance, or a lagging indicator. The Quality Review deals with how well processes and systems are established in the school and consequently is an indicator of a school's capacity to improve, which makes it a leading indicator. The first Quality Review rubric was designed to evaluate how well schools were using data to support school improvement. It had five Quality Statements, and each statement had between four and seven criteria; each criterion was judged on a three-point scale:

- Well developed
- Proficient
- Underdeveloped

All judgments were combined to create an overall outcome for the school using the same three-point scale.

Principals were trained and asked to complete a school self-evaluation with their faculty, using the same rubric, before the visit by an external reviewer. During the Quality Review, which typically involved a site visit of 1 or 2 days, the reviewer gathered evidence related to each of the five statements. The reviewer's judgments were based on evidence collected on site.

High School Choice and Diversity

Before moving on to look at later refinements of the system, we explore the combined impact of two chief elements of Children First reforms on high schools: the introduction of mandatory choice and the drive to replace large low-performing high schools with new small theme-based high schools. At the turn of the millennium, political debate about promoting choice and diversity in education was prominent in the United States and elsewhere.[45] In NYC the shift from centralized control to choice

and diversity of schools under the Children First reform appears to have
been influenced by the following:

- An explicit commitment by Bloomberg and Klein to establish and
  support as many charter schools as possible in NYC.[46]
- The belief that choice and diversity are essential conditions for
  creating a competitive, market-led system of schools.
- The New Century High Schools initiative that was already in
  place at the start of the Children First reforms, replacing large
  failing high schools with smaller schools offering specialized
  programs.[47]
- The remarkable success of the NYC pioneers of school choice in
  Community School District 4 from the 1980s.[48]

In fact, the development of school choice in NYC started before 2002 and
was well under way as Mayor Bloomberg and Chancellor Klein embarked
on the Children First reforms.

Instituting Choice

The most significant contribution of Children First reforms to choice
in NYC was to make high school choice mandatory in 2004. After that, all
8th-grade students faced the paradox of having no choice other than to
choose their high school; the default option of attending their local high
school was removed.[49] And for many students the active choice of attending a local neighborhood high school was eliminated because such schools
no longer existed in some parts of NYC.

The scale and pace of large-high-school closures and small-high-
school openings, supported by the Bill and Melinda Gates Foundation,
increased rapidly under Children First. The Gates Foundation donated
$51.2 million in various grants to create a total of 67 small theme-based
public high schools in NYC. This was a significant contribution that boosted Mayor Bloomberg's intention to open over 200 small high schools.[50]
From 2002–2007 the NYC Department of Education closed 23 large and
mid-sized high schools with graduation rates under 45%; over the following 3 years a further 22 schools were closed. As they were closing these
45 low-performing high schools, the department opened 207 small high
schools mostly in the same buildings to ensure there were sufficient school
places available in the system.[51]

In 2005 the NYC Department of Education combined the administration of closing schools with that responsible for creating new small schools
to form the Office of Portfolio Development, charged with managing the
mix. In order to change the school landscape, as the portfolio expanded, it

also increased diversity by creating boutique schools offering a wide range of specialties. Each small high school enrolls up to 500 students compared with the large high schools of 3,000+ students. Most of these new small nonselective high schools are located in Brooklyn and the Bronx, although they have citywide intakes. They shared the following student characteristics in 2008:[52]

- Over 90% of students are Hispanic or Black.
- Over 80% of students come from low-income families.
- Over 50% of students scored low on 8th-grade proficiency tests in ELA and mathematics.
- Over 25% of students are overage for grade in 8th grade.

A study of 123 small schools of choice (SSCs) in 2008 found that by the 4th year of high school, SSCs increased overall graduation rates by 6.8 percentage points; this represents one-third of the achievement gap between White students and Hispanic or Black students in NYC.[53] The most recently published study of the same schools matched students in SSCs with a control group in other types of NYC public high schools. SSCs boosted graduation rates by 8.6 percentage points.[54]

In 2007 across the city new small high schools consistently achieved higher graduation rates than the large schools they replaced.[55] While this is good news for those students that graduated, we need to be cautious about such comparisons. Obviously, these were not the same students that attended the low-performing large high schools. In a system geared up for free choice, we should not assume we are comparing like with like, based on school buildings. While the building is in the same place, when schools are no longer zoned, the profile of the student intake may change unpredictably.

Impacts of Choice Policy

Diane Ravitch points out the disturbing consequences that closing large high schools had on other schools in the system.[56] A similar pattern of events played out in school after school. As a high school with capacity for 3,000 students closed, it was replaced by four or five small schools that enrolled 500 students each. Where did the other 500 students go? These were more likely to be the lowest-performing and least-motivated students. They turned up at other large high schools and sent those schools into spirals of decline until they were eventually closed; the pattern was repeated time after time.[57] This domino effect was revealed in an analysis of 34 large high schools in Brooklyn, the Bronx, and Manhattan.[58] From

2002 to 2007, 26 of these schools found their enrollments increase from between 150 and 1,100 additional students, while attendance fell in 19 schools and graduation rates dropped in 15. Some of them were among the 200 highest-performing schools exempt from centralization in 2003, with traditions of high academic achievement for Black and Hispanic students.

Klein's response was pure market-based ideology: "Some of those schools managed the challenges and some are not managing the challenges. And those that aren't, we will have to reconstitute."[59] In our dynamic framework, the system's courage to intervene and close schools far outweighed its efforts to build sustainable improvements in low-performing schools. It illustrates Klein's tendency toward extreme push actions, apparently abandoning any attempt to pull people with him.

Even recent history reminds us that markets sometimes become unstable and crash. We point to two directions that the market-based school system in NYC appears to be heading that threaten its sustainability. First, a report in 2012 by the New York City Working Group on School Transformation noted that the market has created a concentration of high-needs students in some schools.[60] The report claimed that the structural remedy of closing schools without a capacity-building strategy had resulted in a growth of struggling schools. This raises questions about the effectiveness of the choice and diversity strategy. We would add that if this growth remains unchecked it may eventually overwhelm the Office of Portfolio Development. There is a lack of balance between the sense of urgency using data to close low-performing schools and the attempts to develop professional power in the same schools. Push actions like closure are easy compared to pulling actions that would improve instruction. Too much push and too little pull creates an illusion of success by moving the underlying problems somewhere else.

Second, there is no doubt that the development of small schools had significant influence on the overall improvement of graduation rates in NYC. Nobody would want to turn the clock back and replace them with huge, low-performing schools. But their inherent characteristic, being small, makes them more fragile than larger schools because they inevitably have less professional capacity. Their success is often dependent on a small, highly committed faculty, and normal turnover is more threatening than it would be in a larger faculty. Two reports draw attention to worrying trends. In a study by the Center for New York City Affairs we learn that both teachers and principals in small schools tend to be much younger and less experienced than average across the city and turnover is higher.[61] And a report from the Annenberg Institute about students enrolled in small high schools found that over time the new small schools' intakes became progressively more disadvantaged.[62] With limited capacity, small schools will be less resilient at dealing with more challenging students, particularly those with special needs or English language learners.[63]

Unintentionally, the market-based school system in NYC appears to be acting in ways that strengthen the links between results and student demographics. A study in 2012 indicates that college readiness by high school students in NYC is very highly correlated with the neighborhood they come from. In particular, the racial composition and average income of a student's home neighborhood are very strong predictors of a student's chance of graduating ready for college.[64] This confirms the findings of another report by the Schott Foundation for Public Education in 2011 that showed a student's opportunity to learn in New York City is largely determined by where he or she lives.[65]

In short, despite the Children First efforts to improve equity through choice, diversity, deregulation, and empowerment, students' educational outcomes are still largely predicted by their home neighborhood. The conundrum seems to be, how can a system that is designed to create winners and losers be relied on to improve equity? It seems more likely to us that those with the wealth and know-how to play the system would benefit. This appears to be borne out by Jennings and Pallas, who report that under the Children First reforms high schools have become more segregated in terms of family income.[66]

Capacity Building

During the centralization phase of Children First there was hefty investment in capacity building to support the authorized curriculum for ELA and mathematics. Top-down professional development was supplemented by school-based literacy and mathematics coaches. With respect to our framework, we recognize this as an attempt to balance push and pull dynamics, so it is worth looking closely at these factors in action. Thus we now consider the strategies used by Children First to increase professional capital following deregulation and empowerment.

When the regional structure was replaced by a controlled market of school support organizations, part of the central budget was devolved to schools. Principals were financially empowered to manage professional learning for their schools by selecting their preferred SSO. At the same time the NYC Department of Education introduced its accountability system designed by Jim Liebman. We have already noted that the design was intended to assist capacity building in schools. The question is, did the strategies (tools) that were used actually generate new skills and commitment necessary for sustained implementation?

Accountability System Tools

Three tools were created with the accountability system and provided to help teachers improve students' achievements: Periodic Assessments, the Achievement Reporting & Innovation System (ARIS), and Inquiry Teams. All three tools were focused on instruction.

Periodic Assessments. Selected and administered by classroom teachers, periodic assessments are formative assessments intended to diagnose what students understand and help teachers to plan how to improve students' learning. Periodic assessments are not intended to grade students, teachers, or schools. They are used when students are ready, and the results help teachers track students' progress at grade level and find any gaps in their learning. The NYC Department of Education provides several options for periodic assessments in English and mathematics from which schools may choose.[67] Schools can also apply to design their own set of assessments.

Achievement Reporting & Innovation System (ARIS). An $80 million online data management system built by IBM, ARIS integrates biographical data about each student with their attendance and achievements in all forms of assessments. It was designed to provide student assessment data to teachers in an easily accessible form. Its primary purpose was to help teachers diagnose their students' learning and bring more precision to instruction. For example, after each periodic assessment ARIS generates an item-by-item analysis of what each student does and does not understand. It was also intended that teachers would share good ideas about students' achievement and create an online professional learning community.[68] A parent link was developed later (2009) that gives parents restricted access to their own children's achievement profile. ARIS access points were set up in public libraries.

Teachers can cut and slice the data in many ways. They can check on the progress of any group of students in their school and compare it with similar groups in other schools. And so can the Office of Accountability. ARIS provides real-time information about which schools, principals, and teachers are performing up to expectations. It may be that this more threatening function, in addition to the breathtaking price tag, created resentment and reluctance among teachers and principals to engage with the system. It didn't help that this was another top-down initiative to which teachers, principals, and the community had no input at the design stage. Even with the best system in the world, expect problems if you push it on people without attempting to pull them along. In many ways ARIS was ahead of its time, but it now appears that time is catching up, and New York State has developed a system that will replace it.[69]

Inquiry Teams (Children First Intensive). Unlike Periodic Assessments, which are resource materials, or ARIS, which is a web-based information system, the Inquiry Team is a collaborative process that teachers engage with to gain deeper insights into why some students are not making expected progress.[70] The Inquiry Team process works on the assumption that in any school there will be some students who are not keeping pace with the rest. The collaborative inquiry is a sustained investigation by a small team of teachers into why specific students are falling behind. It brings teachers together to identify those students and analyze all the performance assessment data available to find gaps in their learning. It increases the professional capacity of teachers to analyze data and empowers them to take action across the school in order to close achievement gaps. They plan together how best to fill those gaps and take action to help the students catch up. After several cycles of investigation and action, the collaborative inquiry process also strengthens the school's leadership capacity.

The Inquiry Team approach developed from a program designed by Liz Gewirtzman at Baruch College. It was piloted in the Autonomy Zone during 2004–2005, scaled up to more than 300 schools in the Empowerment Zone in 2006–2007, then refined and launched systemwide the following year as the Children First Intensive (CFI) inquiry initiative.[71] Of all the Children First reforms, the Inquiry Team or CFI offered the most potential in terms of pulling teachers along, increasing professional power and improving students' achievements. Unfortunately, it was severely hampered by pushy implementation.

The timing was unfortunate, and implementation set off along a rocky road. In 2007–2008 schools were reeling from the second system upheaval in 5 years as the regional structure that they were only just getting accustomed to was replaced by school support organizations. At the same time, they were facing their second Quality Review with the report from the first one already posted on the NYC Department of Education website (schools. nyc.gov/Accountability/tools/review/default.htm). And the first Progress Reports, culminating in single-letter school grades, were published. Inquiry Teams were perceived paradoxically as another top-down initiative in the new empowerment era. The department exacerbated that feeling by adding the work of a school's Inquiry Team to the Quality Review rubric. SSOs were reluctant to push the process, fearing that principals would see them as an arm of the department.[72]

An early evaluation in 2008 reported that 54% of schools completed a full inquiry during 2007–2008 and this had risen to 75% during the fall of 2008.[73] This research does not distinguish between schools that went through the motions and those that accomplished more profound inquiry that closed achievement gaps. The question is not how many schools were engaged in full inquiry, but rather what exactly were the new competencies in question, did people (individuals and groups) acquire and put them into practice, and did they in turn get better results. A further study by Marian Robinson looked in more depth at a sample of 13 schools to discover the conditions, structures, relationships, and leadership practices that support teacher participation in CFI inquiry. Even in such a small sample there was wide variation in success.[74]

By 2010, there was wide deviation in the implementation of CFI. At one extreme was a small group of schools involved in the pilot with 5 years of successful iterations developing robust inquiries, and at the other extreme, schools that had lacked leadership and/or support and carried out rituals through assigned team meetings that had no impact on students' achievement. The remaining schools lay somewhere in between. Joan Talbert studied a sample of 14 schools that originally worked on collaborative inquiry with Baruch College and another sample of over 70 schools from one of the SSOs that had no prior involvement with Inquiry Teams until CFI.[75] Her conclusion was that the track records of schools that had successfully implemented the process indicated that inquiry-based reform will pay off in the long run for most NYC schools. These schools changed practices to support struggling students and closed achievement gaps. To shift the process from surface rituals to deep meaningful inquiry relied on a skilled facilitator, assessment protocol, and real commitment by the school principal to inquiry-led reform and teacher leadership. It seems to us that getting teachers better at data analysis is a fair start, but there is still some way to go before effective CFI is closing achievement gaps in NYC.[76]

Teacher Recruitment and Retention

So far we have considered the processes and tools used by Children First to improve the teaching capacity of its workforce through job-embedded professional learning. We now consider another two important aspects to capacity building: recruiting better teachers in the first place and retaining good teachers in the system. In doing so, we draw largely on a detailed study by Margaret Goertz, Susanna Loeb, and Jim Wycoff.[77]

Teacher recruitment was a problem before the Children First reforms. From 1995–2002 about half of all new teachers in NYC were uncertified.[78] Furthermore, evidence shows that more experienced and better qualified teachers were less likely to teach in schools with higher proportions of students from low-income families.[79] In the decade before Children First, teachers' starting salaries in NYC were 20% lower than the surrounding suburban school districts and did not keep pace with inflation. Working conditions were poor in many schools, and excessively bureaucratic procedures obstructed efforts to recruit the best applicants. The processes for removing ineffective and low-performing teachers were so difficult and time-consuming that most principals were discouraged from even trying.[80] Goertz et al. remind us that although NYC faced these challenges, there were outstanding teachers and schools within the system. Unfortunately, they were not widely distributed, particularly among the neediest students.

Starting from a fairly low base, Children First crafted a strategy to improve recruitment and retention of good teachers; the strategy evolved over the years. As with the structural reforms already described, the approach was to tighten central control at first, then devolve responsibility, with accountability, to schools as appropriate programs were established.

By 2008, teachers' starting salaries increased by 35% over inflation, making NYC more competitive in terms of recruitment. Other financial incentives were introduced to attract teachers to work in the most challenging schools. To increase the supply of better qualified teachers, the NYC Department of Education developed the New York City Teaching Fellows program. This very selective program prepares teachers for high-need schools and supports them through ongoing study for master's degrees at city universities. As a result, the gap in teacher qualifications between low- and high-poverty schools has declined. A study of the different teacher preparation pathways showed that teachers from the Teaching Fellows program became more effective than uncertified teachers and as good as traditionally college-trained teachers.[81] As this fresh supply increased, the number of uncertified teachers dropped, eventually to zero by 2006. These improvements in qualified teachers, especially in high-need schools, appeared to increase student achievement.[82] To deepen and sustain this individual teacher effect, schools must improve their cultures as well, that is, they must become well-led, focused, and collaborative schools, with teachers supporting and learning from one another. If this does not happen, good teachers will not stay for long.

Under Children First, the Office of Teacher Recruitment and Quality streamlined the recruitment process while making it much more rigorous. Until the credit crunch in 2008, the most talented applicants were guaranteed jobs within the NYC public school system and school principals hired teachers directly from this pool.

Goertz et al. regard school leadership as the most important working condition that influences teacher retention.[83] Developing leadership capacity was a high priority for Children First, and establishing the New York City Leadership Academy was one of the earliest initiatives. Founded in 2003, the Leadership Academy is an independent nonprofit organization that recruits and prepares aspiring public school leaders to become principals in high-need NYC schools.[84] By 2012, 17% of NYC principals had been through the academy's Aspiring Principals Program (APP), developed by CEO Sandra Stein. An evaluation by New York University in 2009 found that in the initial years of their leadership, elementary and middle school APP principals had comparable or better growth trends in student test scores than comparison principals who had not attended the Leadership Academy.[85] Again we put on our collective capacity hat. Michael Fullan has just completed a book called *The Principal: Three Keys for Maximizing Impact,*[86] in which he makes the claim that school principals are being whipsawed (depending on the system and on the period) from expectations that they will be autonomous saviors to requirements that box them into a narrow role of focusing on instructional practices of individual teachers.[86] In either case, autonomous change agents or micromanagers, they will fail to develop the professional capital of the group that would generate far more impact on student learning.

Throughout the Children First reform era Mayor Bloomberg advocated bonus pay to recruit, retain, and reward high-performing teachers working in the city's most challenging schools. While merit pay is common in the private sector, its introduction in the public school system was resisted by teacher unions. In 2007, however, a deal was brokered with the United Federation of Teachers (UFT) in NYC.[87] Under the deal, 200 of the city's high-needs schools were eligible for up to $20 million in bonuses ($3,000 per teacher) paid for meeting school performance targets in students' test scores. Successful schools had to form a teacher committee to decide how to share the bonus among staff. In return for this agreement, the union secured important retirement benefits for the teachers' pension plan. An evaluation of the scheme by the RAND Corporation in 2011 compared the performance of 200 schools that qualified for the bonus with a control group of schools. The study found no positive effect on either student performance or teachers' attitudes toward their jobs.[88] Following the report, the scheme was permanently discontinued during budget cuts, although the search continues for a merit-pay model that works.[89] It is important to note that merit pay is a pull factor that is based on *extrinsic rewards,* while it is well established that the *intrinsic rewards* of accomplishing something personally meaningful and working with peers on crucially important matters has far more pull, especially among professionals.

Overall, under Children First, recruitment procedures are more efficient. Alternative certification routes have purged uncertified teachers from the system, and greater rigor has improved the qualifications of the teaching force. Evidence indicates that this has improved students' test scores. Keeping good teachers in high-poverty schools remains an issue, but there has been a modest decrease in the attrition rate. And according to the Learning Environment survey, teachers find schools more attractive workplaces.[90] The status quo was successfully challenged because Bloomberg worked with the unions to create a commonly owned strategy, but we would say the gains are not sustainable because there was insufficient attention to building capacity among groups of teachers and principals.

Community Engagement and Parental Involvement

Immediately before Children First, schools were administered by 32 community school districts. These were arranged geographically and each elected school board, representing parents and the local community, hired a superintendent, set priorities, and implemented its own policies. We have already noted the inequities that developed out of this discredited system, which eventually led to mayoral control, centralizing power and shifting authority away from parents and the community. While centralization followed by school empowerment sidestepped resistance to reforms, it also fractured community engagement.[91]

Instead of engaging with the community, Children First promoted parental involvement at the school level by hiring parent coordinators in every school. Yet there were tensions associated with the position because the principals hired the parent coordinators, which constrained their role as parent advocate. Some parents considered them a blockage between principals and parents.[92] After the second system reorganization in 2007, which abolished the 10 regional divisions, the NYC Department of Education established the Office for Family Engagement and Advocacy (OFEA) to help parents by connecting them with appropriate services if they had grievances. Parent coordinators from schools were trained by, and initially reported to, the OFEA, thereby creating another tension for parent coordinators between their school and the NYC Department of Education. Pressures on the parent coordinators emerged in 2011 when it was reported that the NYC Department of Education wanted them to lobby other parents to support the department's planned school closures.[93]

Parents were routinely surveyed as part of the accountability reform introduced by Liebman. As we noted earlier, their views were added to those of students and teachers in the Learning Environment section of each school's annual Progress Report. The Children First approach to parents as consumers who exercise their democracy through school choice and provide feedback to the center that controls the system was at odds with state legislature.[94] For example, New York State law required every school to appoint a School Leadership Team (SLT) consisting of a 50:50 mix of parents and staff to set the school's priorities. And each district was required to elect a Community Education Council to establish policies and objectives for elementary and middle schools under its jurisdiction. These structures, which grew out of a more active realization of community engagement, were effectively disempowered by Children First reforms.[95] With mayoral control of the school system limited by legislation and due to end in 2009, opposition became more prominent during the buildup to the 2009 mayoral election.

A further twist to the 2009 election was added when Mayor Bloomberg announced his intention to modify the city's two-term limit law so that he could stand for re-election to a third term on the grounds that his financial business experience was essential for the city at the time of the worldwide financial crisis.[96] This special dispensation had broad support on the City Council and was approved, but only for a possible third term.

In August 2009 the New York State Senate voted 47–8 in favor of extending mayoral control of NYC schools for a further 6 years with the division along racial lines as most senators who criticized the administration were Black, while those in support were White.[97] Although the mayor retained control of the Panel for Educational Policy, the NYC Department of Education conceded ground by passing the analysis of financial and achievement data to an independent body and by agreeing to the following restrictions concerning future school closures: 6 months' notice, an impact statement, and a public hearing. Seemingly innocuous at the time, these concessions later caused serious aggravation for the administration's reform implementation.

Mayor Bloomberg's Third Term

In November 2009 Mayor Bloomberg was elected for a third term 51%–46%. The close result surprised the mayor's followers, who expected an 18-point gap. Exit polls suggested that voters resented Bloomberg's legal manipulations to enable him to run for a third term and the $102 million campaign fund from his personal fortune, viewed as excessive compared to his opponent's.[98] Bloomberg's supporters were more concerned with the doomed economy and job creation than the mayor's education track record.[99]

As we have shown, during Bloomberg's first mayoral term from 2001–2005, Children First reforms were characterized by centralization, as Chancellor Klein took control of the school system and abolished the 32 community school districts. Through Bloomberg's second term from 2005–2009, Chancellor Klein displayed continuing push-oriented leadership by empowering school principals, increasing accountability for schools and principals, closing large failing schools, and creating a diverse portfolio of schools, including charter schools, deliberately designed to encourage competition. By comparison, Bloomberg's third term, 2009–2013, was more reactive than proactive and appeared to be chaotic at times as it felt the backlash from the community over the lack of balance in push–pull dynamics. Education reform under its banner of "Raising the Bar" was also hindered by a series of unplanned leadership changes. On a larger note, we would say that the whole strategy was inherently unstable because push factors dominated the 2002–2009 period without a corresponding buildup of pull factors of capacity building and collaboration that would have generated more ownership on the ground.

The frustrations and simmering resentments of parents and community advocates over the NYC Department of Education's controversial policy on school closures erupted at a PEP meeting in January 2010. This explosion had a long fuse lit back in 2004 when Bloomberg refused to tolerate any opposition in the PEP. Two thousand people turned out and 300 speakers, mostly critical of the administration's proposals to close 19 failing schools, kept the noisy public meeting going for over 8 hours.[100] While the foregone conclusion was to approve the closures, given the mayor's built-in majority of supporters on the PEP, it didn't end there. The seemingly innocuous conditions about school closures introduced by the State Senate when mayoral control was extended in 2009 sparked off frustration for the administration. Opponents argued that the PEP vote was improper because the impact statements about school closures were vague and failed to respond to concerns raised by the community. This led to litigation in the State Supreme Court in March 2010, where Justice Joan B. Lois blocked the department's planned closure of these schools.[101]

A decision to appeal this judgment created logistical uncertainty for the department's plans to open 10 new public schools and 4 charter schools and move 2 existing public schools into the buildings occupied by the 19 schools scheduled for closure.[102] Despite this delay while waiting for the appeals court's decision, the administration published plans to close another 16 schools in the following school year.[103] Delay turned to disarray when the appeals court agreed unanimously that the department must keep the 19 failing schools open.[104] Seemingly undeterred, in October 2010 the department added another 12 schools to its proposed closure list, making a total of 47 to be phased out.[105] Another major confrontation with parents and community organizations opposing school closures was looming for a series of public hearings in February 2011.

Meanwhile, more structural upheaval was implemented in spring 2010: the third systemic reorganization under Children First reforms. As before, the new structure was developed and tested by Eric Nadelstern with schools in the Empowerment Support Organization.[106] The five integrated service centers described earlier to provide back-office functions for the school support organizations (SSOs) were abolished. These functions were transferred to 59 Children First Networks (CFNs) across the system and combined with instructional support. Schools were responsible for choosing which CFN they would join, although most networks already existed under the SSO umbrellas. Each CFN supports about 25 schools, a mix of elementary, middle, and high schools that share common curriculum ideas or pedagogy; they are not geographically based.[107] A CFN has about 15 staff, typically a leader and deputy, five instructional coaches, five operations experts, and three student and family services officers. The 59 CFNs are affiliated with one of five clusters, which are the relics of former SSOs. The reasoning for this change was twofold. First, it brought all the support functions for each school to a single organization that is responsible directly to the schools in the network. And second, it cut costs. As of November 2013, these were the current school support arrangements. Overlying this support structure there are 32 community school district superintendents (based on the original geographically based districts) and six high school superintendents responsible for hiring and firing school principals and carrying out their performance management reviews.[108]

Two notable promotions were made in April 2010 to Chancellor Klein's leadership team at the NYC Department of Education. Eric Nadelstern was appointed deputy chancellor for school support and instruction, overseeing the structure he designed and we outlined above. Nadelstern was widely seen as a successor to Chancellor Klein. Santiago Taveras, who a year earlier had been appointed deputy chancellor of teaching and learning, was put in charge of community engagement.[109] Closure of the division that supervised school curriculum and teacher training in the department was the final stage of the shift from centralized control of the curriculum to school empowerment. Both Nadelstern and Taveras were lifelong educators who had worked their way up through the ranks in NYC schools. Former teachers and principals, they were appointed to the administration before Bloomberg's election in 2001. Their continued promotion through the Children First era is a tribute to their knowledge, skills, and expertise. Nadelstern initiated the Empowerment Zone through which many reforms developed. Taveras was responsible for designing and implementing the Quality Review. When Chancellor Klein left NYC, he publicly acknowledged he was leaving his successor with the best education department in the country.

Chancellor Klein's Resignation and the Aftermath

Chancellor Klein resigned in November 2010. Mayor Bloomberg immediately appointed Cathleen P. Black, a publishing executive with no previous education experience, as chancellor. Approval by State Commissioner David Stein was subject to Black's appointing an experienced educator as her chief deputy to supervise instruction.[110] Klein stayed on to the end of the year to ease the leadership succession.

Black's appointment surprised everyone in the NYC Department of Education and across the city.[111] Those in the leadership did not know Klein was resigning, let alone that Bloomberg had picked his replacement. Even Klein did not know who his successor would be until the day before Bloomberg's announcement. The secrecy over the appointment was to avoid the inevitable destabilization and loss of focus during a lengthy recruitment process. The chancellor-in-waiting announced the appointment of Shael Polakow-Suransky as her principal deputy in December 2010, to comply with the State Commissioner's approval of her own appointment.[112] Polakow-Suransky, who was mentored by Nadelstern, introduced Inquiry Teams and had taken over the Office of Accountability after Liebman returned to his faculty post at Columbia Law School in 2009.

Chancellor Black started work in January 2011. Her leadership succession came at a difficult time, when public relationships between the NYC Department of Education and the community were openly hostile over the department's policy to close large high schools with low graduation rates and replace them with a mix of small public high schools and charter schools. The department's closure plans had already been stalled in 2010. Black's first priority was to continue the department's school portfolio development. The opposition, encouraged by their success in 2010, was prepared for another huge confrontation at a series of public meetings scheduled for February 2011. Before that, though, the department's leadership suffered a major blow when Nadelstern announced his retirement to take effect at the end of January 2011.[113]

Black's induction was more of a trial by ordeal than a honeymoon period that leaders typically enjoy when starting in a new organization. As expected, thousands of noisy protesters turned out at two public meetings to voice objections to the planned school closures. Although everyone knew the outcome of the meetings would be to approve the closure of 22 struggling schools (of which 15 were reprieved the previous year), the frenzy and the personal nature of the verbal attacks on Chancellor Black were surprising.[114] A tiny groan from Black in response to the angry protests was seized on as a sign of disrespect by some of the crowd. While closing schools will always be difficult, the lynch mob fury at these public meetings seemed to be fostered in part by the mayor's total control of the system without adequate release valves for the community to express its opinions, let alone shape policy.[115]

Chancellor Black's bumpy ride continued in April 2011 when Deputy Chancellor Santiago Taveras resigned, after 22 years of service with the department. Taveras was well liked and respected, particularly by the community, who could identify with him because of his NYC background.[116] His departure followed other long-serving leaders in the department after

Black's appointment. Three days later, Mayor Bloomberg fired Chancellor Black and appointed Deputy Mayor Dennis M. Walcott as Schools Chancellor.[117] Black's removal after 3 months in the job was a huge setback for the Children First reforms in Bloomberg's third term. A public opinion poll in May 2011 expressed widespread disapproval of the mayor's handling of education, reversing the results of a poll taken just before he was re-elected.[118]

Chancellor Walcott's Appointment

Chancellor Walcott was well placed to hit the ground running. As the mayor's deputy for education throughout the Children First reforms, he needed no introduction to the chancellor's job. He knew everyone he needed to know in both the city and state education departments. Better still, he was respected in both.[119] Walcott was born in NYC, attended public school there, and then taught kindergarten in the city. He was better placed than most to connect with the community and stabilize the mayor's education reforms through the remainder of his term. In the earlier phases of Children First, Deputy Mayor Walcott was comfortable in his role of mediating disputes, calming tensions, and endlessly listening.[120] At the start of the new school year in September 2011, Walcott announced that it would be a year focused on public relations, not policy shifts: "I want to have both theoretical and practical discussions about what we need to do in our schools without the anger and acrimony that's occurred in the past."[121] This was an immediate signal that the new chancellor intended to restore some balance in terms of our push–pull dynamics.

In July 2011 the NYC Department of Education reached an important agreement with the United Federation of Teachers (UFT) to implement a state teacher evaluation system in persistently low-achieving schools.[122] The agreement enabled NYC to draw $65 million in federal School Improvement Grants to help transform 33 schools that otherwise faced closure. Under this federal program schools had to follow one of four prescribed models for school improvement. The state evaluation system graded teachers in four categories—highly effective, effective, developing, and ineffective—but it only applied to teachers in schools following this federal program. Elsewhere in the city, teachers were still rated as either satisfactory or unsatisfactory and the department continued negotiating with the UFT to renew the citywide teacher evaluation system.

Improving the quality of teaching in schools covered two of the mayor's five key priorities in his penultimate State of the City address in January 2012. In his speech the mayor outlined new methods of implementing merit pay and also paying off student loans to attract top graduates to teach in NYC. Despite the agreement reached in July 2011 over a new teacher evaluation system in struggling schools, the administration and the UFT had reached a stalemate that prevented the department from drawing the $65 million in federal grants. So this came high on his list of priorities.

Teacher Evaluations

Merit pay, charter schools, and using student test scores for teacher evaluations were all controversial policies. Bloomberg drew criticism from city officials likely to run for mayor in 2013, who described his presentation of the education proposals as "needlessly provocative" or "very aggressive."[123] Bloomberg was continuing the pushy approach adopted by Klein, although he was more concerned with the financial crisis than implementation of education reforms, leaving that in the reliable hands of Chancellor Walcott. The stalemate over teacher evaluations was connected to a 3-year dispute over teacher quality ratings based on students' grades in standardized tests. These were developed by Chancellor Klein in 2008 as a way of helping teachers to understand their own performance. Every teacher from 4th to 8th grade who taught English and/or mathematics received a "teacher data report" that classified them as above average, average, or below average, according to a statistical analysis of their students' test scores from one year to the next.[124] The report isolated contributions each teacher made to students' progress in their class and judged that relative to other teachers with similar students. At the time, Klein agreed with the UFT that the results would not be published or used to influence job evaluations, pay, or promotions. This was reinforced by state legislation that banned the use of test data for teacher evaluations until June 2010 at the earliest.[125]

By September 2009, some 12,000 teachers who had taught English or mathematics for 2 years in 4th to 8th grades received their teacher data reports, but none were published.[126] With President Obama and education secretary Arne Duncan pushing states to use student performance data to evaluate teachers, New York City was at the center of the national debate because it had developed a system to achieve that but was prevented from using it by state legislation. In November 2009 Mayor Bloomberg made a speech in Washington announcing that student test scores would be used in NYC to determine which teachers would gain tenure.[127] In May 2010 the UFT reached agreement with the New York State Education Department to base 40% of a teacher's evaluation on student test scores.[128]

A study by Sean Corcoran from the Annenberg Institute looked in detail at the Teacher Data Initiative in NYC and considered whether teachers can and should be evaluated by their students' test scores.[129] He concluded that while it may be highly desirable to have a measure that isolates the teacher's contribution from all other factors, the value-added measures currently available were crude indicators for this purpose. The measures were only used for ELA and mathematics between 4th and 8th grades, so they did not apply to all teachers. And those teachers identified by the teacher data reports as consistently effective or ineffective, the top and bottom 5%, were already highly visible using other evaluation methods.

Soon after teachers received their data reports, various news media made freedom of information requests for access to the data. This wound up in court in January 2011, where a Manhattan judge ruled that the NYC Department of Education may release the data to the public.[130] The department agreed to withhold the data until the UFT appeal had been heard. While the appeals were working their way through the courts, in September 2011 the NYC Department of Education announced a surprising twist to the tale by saying it was going to cease issuing teacher data reports. The reason given was that the state education department was planning to introduce its own teacher evaluation system based partly on student test scores.[131] Duplication in NYC was a needless expense, and the decision was welcomed by the UFT. Even so, the union's appeals failed and publication of the teacher data was only stalled until February 2012.[132]

Composure and Appeasement

Chancellor Walcott continued his unobtrusive implementation of Children First policies. A charter school was placed on the closure list in January 2012 despite achieving three C grades in its Progress Reports. The message from the chancellor seemed to be that charter schools were meant to be outstanding and mediocrity is not good enough.[133] In April 2012 seven schools were removed from the closure list because they received A or B grades, and another two got an 11th-hour reprieve from the chancellor because they could gather sufficient evidence to show they were improving. New York State Chancellor Merryl Tisch said the city's decision was honorable.[134] Despite these last-minute acquittals, the NYC Department of Education still closed 24 schools. Chancellor Walcott continued to repair the damage that had been caused through the first two phases of Children First through too much push and insufficient pull, by introducing a more balanced set of purposeful actions.

We end our narrative in 2012 after a decade of Children First reforms. Following the mayoral elections in November 2013, the school system will be Bill de Blasio's responsibility until at least 2015, when the New York State senate has to decide whether to renew mayoral control of education in the city. This case story deals with the key educational changes over a decade that created the situation the new mayor faces.

New York City Student Achievement, 2002–2012

We now examine more closely the outcomes of those education changes in terms of students' achievements. We say in advance that there are myriad assessment tests that, taken together and given inconsistencies, make it very difficult to draw clear conclusions. This means that it is equally difficult for those in the schools, for parents, or for third parties to be clear about the overall impact. This lack of clarity with respect to results is another indicator of problems that surround the decade of reform we studied. That being said, we present below the findings from our analysis of standardized test results from elementary and middle schools, together with graduation rates from high schools.

Grades 3–8

From 2002–2005, NYC had its own tests for English language arts (ELA) and mathematics in Grades 3, 5, 6, and 7. New York State tests were mandated for ELA and math in Grades 4 and 8. From 2005 onward, New York State tests were mandated for ELA and math in all Grades 3–8 to comply with federal requirements under NCLB legislation. Consequently, state tests in Grades 4 and 8 are the only continuous lines of data across the decade. Results from 2002–2005 are premature for our purposes because they could only capture the possible effects of the first phase of reforms. State tests place students at four performance levels where Level 1 is low and 4 is high; Level 3 is considered to be the proficiency level at each grade.

There are continuous data sets for 2006–2012 for New York State tests. There is a huge dip in all test results in 2010 because the scale marks were adjusted after 2009 and students had to achieve higher scores for each level. Consequently, the drop from 2009 to 2010 is mainly due to tougher marking. In effect, from 2010 they are different scales, and this makes it impossible to compare results in 2012 directly with those in 2009 or earlier.[135]

Thus we need to interpret two separate series of data, 2006–2009 and 2010–2012, presented in Figure 2.2. Two points emerge: (1) Results steadily improved in both series and in both ELA and math; (2) Performance in math is better than ELA; in 2002 there were significantly fewer students proficient in math compared with ELA but they were measured with different tests.

Although there may be an improving trend in state tests, the bottom line is that in 2012 less than half of the students in Grades 3–8 could read and write fluently. When we look at the performances of different ethnic groups, English language learners, and students with disabilities, there

Figure 2.2. Percentage of NYC Students in Grades 3–8 at Levels 3 and 4 n New York State Tests in ELA and Math

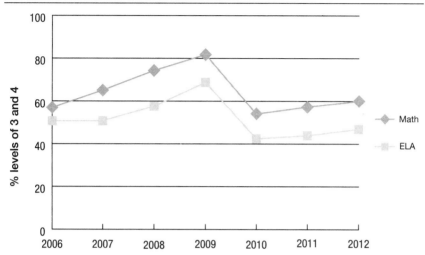

are wide gaps in performance levels that are not closing (see online Appendix A at www.tcpress.com for a detailed analysis).

High School Graduation Rates

Graduation rates across high schools have been published by the NYC Department of Education since 2002 and by the Board of Education before that. Domanico reported that only 50% of students in NYC graduated in 2002, and graduation rates had been flat since the 1990s.[136] This is the only measure we have at the start of the Children First reforms, and we consider the trend in the NYC calculated rate since then, for historical purposes, as evidence of the impact of the reforms.[137]

The New York State Education Department uses a different method to calculate the graduation rate, one that includes all special education and disabled students. We have also collected these data from 2005 and report them, without getting sidetracked by the different statistical methods (see Figure 2.3).

From 2002–2010 there is a significant improvement, using the city calculation, of about 20 percentage points. The trend is similar using the state calculation method, with a gain of 15 points from 2005, although there are fewer graduates. Since 2008, students have been able to attend a summer school and graduate in August. We include those data separately to clarify the situation. All further analyses of graduation rates in this chapter use the state's calculated rate for students graduating in June of their 4th year

Figure 2.3. High School Graduation Rates for NYC, Comparing 4th-Year State Method with City Method

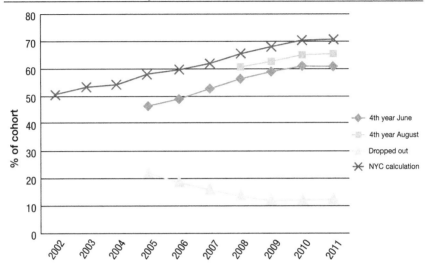

in high school. These data are for public schools only; they do not include charter schools.

The state graduation rate has three components: a local diploma, a Regents diploma, and an advanced Regents diploma. To graduate with a Regents diploma, a student needs to score at least 65% in five Regents examinations, including English, math, and science. For an advanced diploma students must also score 65% in another five Regents examinations, including a foreign language. The local diploma is gradually being phased out and the requirements for a local diploma after 2007 became more demanding, as shown in Table 2.1.

Table 2.1. New York State Graduation Requirements for Local Diplomas, 2008–2011

Year	Local Diploma Requirement
2008	5 Regents examinations with 55% or higher
2009	2 Regents exams at 65% or higher plus 3 Regents exams at 55% or higher
2010	3 Regents exams at 65% or higher plus 2 Regents exams at 55% or higher
2011	4 Regents exams at 65% or higher plus 1 Regents exam at 55% or higher

Figure 2.4. Composition of High School Graduation Rates in NYC, 2005–2012

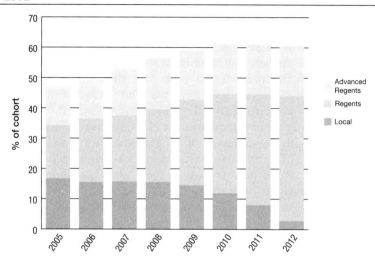

Although the state has raised the bar for graduate requirements since 2008, NYC has sustained its graduation rate (see Figure 2.4). From 2012 on, a Regents Diploma is the minimum graduation requirement. In 2002, only 19% of students in NYC passed five Regents exams with 65% or higher; in 2009, 57% met this requirement. This suggests a significant improvement in high school graduations in NYC during the decade of Children First reform up to 2009.

A detailed analysis of the learning trajectories of a whole NYC student cohort (77,500 students) from 9th grade in 2005 to graduation in 2009 was completed by Ready, Hatch, Warner, and Chu at Teachers College.[138] As this was the last cohort to show significant improvement under Children First, this report is a valuable insight. It reveals that the historic inequities we explore in Chapter 1 remain major challenges in NYC.

These increases in graduation rates prompted questions and specula-tion about the accuracy of these data. Diane Ravitch notes that "the gradu-ation rates were even more malleable than the test scores as there were so many ways to adjust them up or down."[139] One aspect concerned students who were classified as "discharged" from high schools: These are students who transfer to another school within or beyond NYC. They are removed from the school roll, and if they don't show up in another NYC school, then they are also removed from the cohort. Students who drop out are still counted in the cohort, so if students leaving school are classified as discharged, rather than dropping out, then that would affect the gradu-ation rate for both the school and also across the system. The issue was investigated by the New York City Independent Budget Office (IBO).[140] The IBO reports that if these students were classified as dropouts it would have the effect of reducing the graduation rate by 0.6%, which would not be a significant difference, but the whole exercise is an example of confusion and mistrust in the system.

Ravitch also exposed the dubious system of credit recovery, which one high school principal referred to as "the dirty little secret of high schools."[141] Credit recovery allows students who fail to complete a course to gain a credit by presenting an independent, unmonitored project, or by attending extra sessions. Moreover, many of those who did graduate were unable to cope with the demands of college education—a fact acknowledged by the NYC Department of Education when it switched attention from graduation to college readiness as the system measure. The whole issue of college readiness is examined in detail by Siskin.[142]

To summarize, we note that graduation rates increased from 2002 to 2012, but the improvement has been confused by four factors:

1. Different measures used by the NYC Department of Education and New York State
2. Changing graduation requirements
3. Dubious practices in schools and the system
4. Shift in policy from graduation to college readiness

The lack of significant improvement in graduation rates since 2009 puts a big question mark over the success of high school closures and the portfolio approach to high school choice.

We also analyzed National Assessment of Educational Performance (NAEP) results, state tests, and graduation rates, calculated by New York State for students who graduate by June of their 4th year in high school, according to students' ethnicity and looked at differences for students with disabilities and English language learners. Our analysis shows that the wide achievement gaps remain the same across this decade. (An extended analysis of student achievement data is available in online Appendix A at www.tcpress.com.)

CONCLUSION: THE LIMITS OF RESTRUCTURING

We trained hard . . . but it seemed that every time we were beginning to form into teams we were reorganized. I was to learn later in life that we tend to meet any situation by reorganizing, and what a wonderful method it can be for creating the illusion of progress while producing confusion, inefficiency, and demoralization. (Gaius Petronious, A.D. 66)

We conclude by referring to Michael Bloomberg's vision for the education system that he articulated to the NYC Council Committee on Education in 2002. In terms of raising the bar, he said he was seeking an education system that "expects students to meet high standards for educational achievement."[143]

Our evaluation confirms that the Children First reforms certainly have made high standards as a proposition more visible, but whether actual achievement has been accomplished is open to speculation. Manipulation of data during the decade and the lack of transparency over test and graduation data has cast a cloud over what might be a modest improvement. These are the main achievements:

- Graduation rates improved until 2009, then flattened out.
- Proficiency rates in English language arts and mathematics measured by state tests in Grades 3–8 have improved since 2005, and there is evidence that connects these improvements to the Children First reforms.[144] However, average scores were still low in 2012.
- The NAEP surveys indicate that improvements are more secure in 4th grade than 8th grade (see online Appendix A at www.tcpress.com).

For closing the gap, Mayor Bloomberg also said he was seeking a system that provides "a quality education for every student, where results are not a function of student demographics, but are the product of a system that values achievement by all students."[145] Our analysis of all the test scores and graduation data shows that the reforms have done little, so far, to create greater equality. Wide gaps remain between the performances of different ethnic groups at all levels. The reforms have made no apparent impact. Students with disabilities and English language learners perform at very low levels, and in some instances the gap is increasing.

When you take the decade as a whole, perhaps the most revealing question as you think of the roller coaster of reform is this: What was it like to be a principal, teacher, parent, student during this decade? We said in Chapter 1 that a combination of push and pull dynamics—creating a commonly owned strategy to challenge the status quo, using achievement data as urgent motivators to improve instruction, and having the courage to intervene but doing so in ways that sustain improvement—are essential for creating precision, consistency, ownership, and continuous improvement on the ground. New York City schools have achieved pockets of success and debatable overall trends of increased performance, but no evidence of reducing the gap that was at the heart of the reform vision of Children First.

In summary, what we conclude is that there has been an attempt to make accountability systematic, but with no corresponding strategy to develop and leverage capacity building. We would also conclude that with constant structural reorganizations, continuous ambiguity about the reliability of results, and pockets of capacity building and good professional learning that were never converted to new patterns of lasting culture, there is an absence of ownership (or even clarity) about the reforms. The result is that little ownership of the reform strategies has been established; or, to state it differently, there is no basis for sustainability of even the good parts of the reform activity.

Restructuring has prevailed over reculturing. Capacity building has been ad hoc and noncontinuous. A culture of collaborative relationships focusing on ongoing improvements has failed to be established, except in small pockets. Most discouraging, we would have to say, there is no greater clarity about what to do in the next phase of reform as a new mayor takes over. Hidden within the reform efforts over the past decade is a great deal of experience and related capacity building. The next phase should be to leverage these qualities for systemwide reform. We make some suggestions for big-city reform in the final chapter of the book. In conclusion, given the widespread disgruntlement in and about the system, and given the lack of clarity and ownership about what should be done next, in a very real sense the new mayor will need to start from scratch in formulating a strategy for the next decade.

CHAPTER 3

Toronto

Success Amidst the Rocks

School improvements in Toronto over the decade of 2002–2012 were part of the Ontario provincial education strategy. The Liberal government in Ontario was elected in 2003 with a mandate to clean up and improve the education system. Over the following decade the government worked in partnership with district school boards and schools to implement a series of reforms that increased student achievement. We begin by investigating the Ontario strategy and providing an outline of the policies as they developed. This provides the big picture of reform. We then explore this landscape to discover how these policies played out in Toronto, the largest and most urban school district in Ontario. We want to point out that coauthor Michael Fullan was involved in designing and implementing the reforms in the Liberal government from 2003 to 2013, as Liberal Premier Dalton McGuinty's Special Adviser in Education.

SETTING THE SCENE

The Greater Toronto Area (GTA) has a growing population that reached 5,583,064 in 2011. There are five separate local government regions that administer their own public services across the GTA: Halton, Peel, York, Durham, and the city of Toronto (see Figure 3.1). The most densely populated is the City of Toronto with 2,615,060 residents.[1] Our study considers the improvements made by the 591 schools in the City of Toronto (hereafter simply called Toronto).

In Canada, education is a provincial responsibility. Ontario is Canada's second-largest province; it covers roughly 1 million square kilometers. That's bigger than Texas and Oklahoma combined and about the same size as France, Belgium, Netherlands, Luxemburg, and Germany joined together. With a population of over 12.8 million, Ontario is home to one-third of all Canadians. The province educates just over 2 million school students, and since 1998 schools have been administered by four separate

Figure 3.1. Map of Greater Toronto Area Showing the Five Municipal Districts. Schools in the City of Toronto Are Administered by the Toronto District School Board.

publicly funded systems: English public, English Catholic, French public, and French Catholic.[2] These four different jurisdictions combine a total of 72 district school boards of which the Toronto District School Board (TDSB), the English public system covering the City of Toronto, is by far the biggest. It is the fourth-largest school district in North America.

There are three main provincial political parties in Ontario: the Conservatives (right of center), Liberals (center-based, veering left or right depending on the times), and the New Democratic Party or NDP (left of center). In the 20-year period from 1990 to the present all three parties were in power sequentially: NDP (1990–1995), Conservatives (1995–2003), and Liberals (2003–present).

Buildup to Reforms

Before exploring how systemwide improvements across Ontario played out in Toronto schools from 2002–2012, we examine the historical context that provided the foundation for the reforms. Today's school boards across Ontario were established in 1997 during the "Common Sense Revolution" of Ontario government led by Mike Harris and the Conservative party. During its tenure, the Harris government cut taxes, minimized government, and demanded massive efficiency savings from public services, including health and education. Over a hectic two terms in office from

1995–2003, they made major changes in schools covering curriculum, testing, finance, governance, accountability, and the teaching profession.[3] Most involved centralizing control to the Ministry of Education and shrinking resources. The teacher unions frequently quarreled with the government over increased workloads and this led to strikes, working to rule (doing no more than the minimum required by the rules of their contract), and lockouts. These actions had a demoralizing effect on the teaching force, while not demonstrating better outcomes for students in schools.[4] Harris resigned as premier midway through the second term, and his successor split the party by trying to regain some of the political center ground. The Liberals, led by Dalton McGuinty, swept to power in 2003 with education as a high priority.

R. D. Gidney traces education policy in Ontario for over half a century after World War II.[5] He shows that aside from their confrontational tactics, many of the Harris government's policies were advocated by previous administrations. They also benefited from and implemented many of the recommendations of the Royal Commission on Learning's *For the Love of Learning*, which was created by the previous government and reported its findings in December 1994 after 2 years' public consultation.[6] For example, all three main political parties supported:

- More accountability through curriculum, assessment, and reporting
- Provincial testing
- Regulation of the teaching profession

These kinds of initiatives weren't confined to Ontario. Similar policy developments marked the end of the 20th century in the United States, the United Kingdom, France, and Japan, as nations shaped their education systems toward global competitiveness.[7]

The 5-year high school program was cut to 4 years in 1999, as exists in almost all other provinces, starting with Grade 9. All students had to follow more of a common core curriculum, and graduation standards were raised. The secondary curriculum was streamlined from three tracks (Basic, General, and Advanced) to two (Academic and Applied), with similar content but at a more theoretical level in the Academic track.

The government set up the Education Quality and Accountability Office (EQAO) in 1996.[8] The testing program has evolved since then, and EQAO currently tests all students in Grades 3 and 6 in reading, writing, and mathematics; Grade 9 students in mathematics; and Grade 10 students in literacy.[9] Passing the Grade 10 Ontario Secondary School Literacy Test (OSSLT) is now a graduation requirement. The Grades 3 and 6 tests started in 1997, and the OSSLT was piloted in 2001 with full implementation in 2002. It should be noted that Ontario, unlike other provinces and many other countries, has no provincial high school exit examinations.

In 1997 the government set up a self-regulating professional agency for teachers called the Ontario College of Teachers (OCT). The OCT licenses, governs, and regulates the Ontario teaching profession in the public interest.[10] The college made a promising start by publishing *Standards of Practice,* but progress on certification was too slow for government ministers.[11] The government intervened in 2001 and outsourced an initial qualifying test for new teachers, the Ontario Teacher Qualifying Test (OTQT), to a testing agency in the United States.[12] Government also required teachers to recertify every 5 years based on evidence of their professional learning. The OCT was authorized to administer the professional learning policy and appraisal process for recertification.

Centralized Control and Cost-Cutting

Other changes introduced during the Common Sense Revolution were more controversial and not supported by other political parties. Most of these were cost-cutting reforms in order to lower taxes. Overall, the Harris government reduced the Ontario education budget by C$5.4 billion in 1997. In January of that year, the government decreased the number of school boards from 129 to 72 by merging smaller boards to create the current district school boards. TDSB was formed by the consolidation of seven urban school boards across the city. In addition, the government reduced the number of trustees on each board and capped their salaries at C$5,000.

The efficiency savings were secured in December 1997 when the government centralized control over all education spending by removing the school boards' power to top up their provincial allocation with local tax revenues. The Ministry of Education applied a funding formula across all four publicly funded education systems and made each board financially accountable for setting a balanced budget within its allocation. This equalization created winners and losers as some boards gained income at others' expense. The full impact was realized in 1998; in order to balance its budget TDSB proposed to close 138 schools.[13] The government was pushed to provide millions of dollars in transitional grants and guarantee 3 years' funding at the 1997–1998 level.

The district school boards and the education ministry continued squabbling about spending cuts over the next 3 years until the government raised the stakes by making it illegal for a school board to operate on a deficit budget. In June 2002 three of the largest boards declared that they were unable to set a balanced budget with their allocations from the funding formula. One of them was TDSB, which set a C$90 million deficit budget. The government responded in two ways. First, it intervened and took control of the three rebel school boards by appointing an "official trustee" in control instead of the elected boards; by September 2002, the ministry was directly responsible for 20% of school students in the province. Second, the government commissioned a review of the provincial funding formula.

Cuts to TDSB education services as a result of reduced provincial funding were extensive and wide-ranging, mostly focused on what the government defined as nonclassroom expenditure.[14] Even with large budget reductions, the ministry supervisor responsible for TDSB was unable to balance the budget and set an illegal deficit budget for 2003 while seeking further reductions. The task force to review the funding formula, led by Professor Mordechai Rozanski, reported to the education ministry in December 2002.[15] The Rozanski report recommended an increase of C$1.8 billion (about 12%) in provincial spending on education and adjustments to update the formula but opposed a restoration of boards' authority to levy taxes.

Reducing school board funding to enable tax breaks was not the only controversial aspect of the Common Sense Revolution. The 1997 legislation also centralized government control over teachers' working conditions such as class sizes, staffing allocations, the length of school year, and time allocations for professional development, lesson preparation, and administrative duties. These are issues that boards and teacher federations had previously negotiated during contractual negotiations. The government immediately added 5 more teaching days to the school year, cut teacher preparation time in half, increased daily instructional time in high schools, and proposed that previous voluntary teacher supervision of extracurricular activities should be mandatory. Education ministers claimed they were increasing the time that teachers spent with students. Teachers argued it was just cutting costs as schools would employ up to 10,000 fewer teachers under the new regulations. Whatever the case, conflict between government and teacher federations erupted and resulted in the worst period of strikes and disruption in the history of Ontario education.[16]

Parents with children in the public education system were alarmed at the polarization and divisions in Ontario education. The government was fighting teachers and school boards; parents were caught up in the melee and struggled to find any objective information about what was happening. Increasing numbers of students moved from the public to the private school system. In 1996 a handful of parents from downtown Toronto were particularly concerned about cuts to education budgets. They formed a community-based organization called People for Education.[17] Their aim is to provide other parents with factual information that they can trust and understand. They survey every school in Ontario each year and collect information about the effects of policy and funding changes in schools. Then they publish an annual report based on the data they have collected themselves. People for Education became a powerful lobby group in education in part because they were one of the few sources of reliable information about the state of the system. Their actions had an important effect leading up to the 2003 election.

Policy Gaps

After separating reforms that were backed by other political parties from those that faced major opposition, we now consider two areas of policy that others advocated but were ignored or rejected by the Common Sense Revolution—early childhood education and support for greater equity. These policy gaps are equally controversial, but complaints were drowned out by the noise coming from other disputes.

We have already noted that the less controversial policies from the Conservative government were ones recommended by the Royal Commission in *For the Love of Learning* published in 1994. In fact, the previous New Democratic Party government had initiated these ideas by establishing committees to plan for secondary curriculum redesign, provincial testing, and the Ontario College of Teachers.[18] In their report the Royal Commissioners acknowledge the Radwanski report published in 1987. George Radwanski, editor of the *Toronto Star* newspaper, was appointed by the Liberal premier in office to advise as to how to reduce the Ontario secondary school dropout rate. Radwanski recommended early childhood education, provincewide standardized testing, a shift to outcomes-based learning, destreaming (detracking) high schools, and a common-core high school curriculum.[19] The Royal Commissioners adapted all of Radwanski's recommendations into their own. The NDP government held back on early childhood education and instead promised to combine day care with early childhood programs for 4- and 5-year-olds.[20] When in office, the Conservatives put early childhood education on hold pending further study.

The Conservatives' Common Sense Revolution was much more active in opposing developments related to equity issues. The ethnic diversity of Toronto grew rapidly in the 1960s and 1970s with the arrival of immigrants from a wide range of non-European countries. The urban boards of education in Toronto responded by promoting the first multicultural and antiracist policies for education in Ontario. By 1990, many urban school boards had adopted racial and cultural equity policies. The NDP government (1990–1995) supported these efforts. An amendment to the 1992 Education Act required all school boards across the province to develop and implement antiracist policies that covered the curriculum, learning materials, assessment practices, and hiring staff. The NDP also made an effort to end streaming in the first year of secondary schooling, an action that was strongly resisted by many teacher and parents. The Conservatives stopped the antiracism initiatives established by the NDP, including those in the Ministry of Education. They abandoned policies aimed at increasing gender equity and deleted references to equity goals such as antiracism and gender equity from ministry goals and curriculum documents.[21]

The Schools We Need

The Conservatives were fighting with teachers on one side and school boards on another. There seemed to be a crisis in public education. Perhaps their self-inflicted coup de grâce was the 2001 bill giving tax credits to parents who send their children to private schools. This was widely perceived as indirect funding for private education while squeezing money out of public schools. In the midst of this fracas and discord, the Ontario Institute for Studies in Education published a short report that summarized the state of education in Ontario with suggestions for a better way forward.[22] A draft of this report was released for discussion in 2002 and tied its recommendations to raising students' achievements, inviting dialogue and debate about the best way to move ahead. The response was overwhelming and encouraging.

> The extent of the response to our first report astonished us. Over the last three months we have heard from a multitude of people. In addition to those who communicated with us individually, we spoke to many groups—in the education sector and in the wider community. The views and concerns of all these people and groups have influenced this final version of the report [*The Schools We Need*]. In general, the reaction confirms the accuracy of our analysis of the negative effects of the Common Sense Revolution on Ontario's schools; a great deal of concern was expressed about the future of public education in the province. This input from our readers has helped us to consolidate our recommendations for a provincial policy framework that helps rather than hinders.[23]

The Schools We Need highlighted four reasons why the Common Sense Revolution failed to raise standards:

1. The sheer number of policies blunts the impact of each.
2. The value of some potentially useful policies has been hampered by poor implementation.
3. Some policies are misguided, at best distracting and at worst harmful.
4. There are serious policy gaps.

It went on to propose five conditions to be established in order to improve schools.

In October 2003 a new Liberal government led by Dalton McGuinty was elected. They built their campaign around the issues raised in *The Schools We Need*, and this election signaled a new direction for education reform in Ontario. It was a moment when "hope and history rhyme."[24]

ONTARIO TRI-LEVEL REFORM

The Liberal government was elected with a majority for its first term of 4 years—2003–2007. In the next election in 2007, McGuinty was re-elected largely on the performance of his government's record in education and helped by a blunder by the leader of the opposition, who made the mistake of proposing funding for all faith-based schools. The public rallied around the concept of public schools and gave McGuinty a second majority in 2007. To round off the story, McGuinty was re-elected in 2011, but with one seat short of a majority, and there ensued some problematic developments between the government and the teacher unions that take us beyond the terms of reference of this chapter, although these disagreements have now been at least temporarily resolved.

Harmony among the three levels in an educational system—school, district, and province—is crucial to achieve large-scale change. Michael Fullan and colleagues made this tri-level proposition before the Ontario reforms were realized.[25] Here we reveal what happened when the idea was deliberately applied to Ontario as a whole.

Ontario Education Strategy: Phase 1

During the 2003 Ontario election the Liberals pledged to improve test scores and lower class sizes in grades K–3. Once the Liberals were elected, their policies were shaped by three general commitments:

- Improve elementary school literacy and numeracy
- Increase high school graduation rates
- Build public confidence in public schools

Premier McGuinty had some favorable conditions to build on. The previous government established provincial testing and an accountability system for district school boards. Although unpopular in some parts of the system, this provided an important yardstick for the ensuing reforms. McGuinty gained immediate widespread approval by repealing legislation around teacher certification and tax credits for private education fees.

The new government followed up its promises with an additional C$2.6 billion commitment to education over its first term in office.[26] They set ambitious targets for the system:

- 90% of classes in grades K–3 to have 20 or fewer children; none more than 23 by 2007
- 75% of Grade 6 students to be proficient in literacy and numeracy by 2008
- 85% of students to graduate from high schools by 2010

Some years before the 2003 election, Dalton McGuinty went to England to learn from the Blair government how they had boosted literacy and numeracy scores across 18,000 elementary schools (see Chapter 4). He discovered that Tony Blair had engaged a team from Ontario, led by Michael Fullan, to evaluate the English national strategies. Back home, McGuinty drew this expertise into his government by appointing Fullan as his adviser. The importance here is that they understood what happened in England; they cherry-picked good ideas and ignored the rest (such as punitive accountability). In particular, the Ontario Strategy, as we refer to it, adapted two of the big ideas from England: *focus* (on a small number of goals) and *capacity building* (coaches, professional learning and support, and instructional materials, including establishing a new unit in the government called the Literacy and Numeracy Secretariat).

One of the components of the English reform that was deliberately eschewed was the combination of target-setting and assertive name-and-shame accountability. In England the strategy generated an obsession with targets. From 1997, schools and districts were compelled to set ever-increasing annual targets for the percentage of students achieving expected levels in national tests. Although schools in England were supported by extra resources, the government regime in our view erred on the push side, which eventually took its toll. The Ontario Strategy didn't follow that track but needed aspirational goals in order to check its progress. In a tri-level reform, where state, districts, and schools work together harmoniously, these were systemwide targets. If the targets were missed, then the system learned and this informed next steps; it didn't point the finger of blame from one level to another. In effect there was equilibrium between challenge and support across the system.

Despite being hampered by low morale and inadequate funding in 2003, schools in Ontario were not in bad shape.[27] There was room for improvement, but there was no widespread concern about chronic school failure. When schools are completely off the rails, they need urgent and clear directions about how to get back on track. That was far from the case in Ontario. Consequently, the new government chose to avoid prescription and top-down mandates.[28] Instead, within the focus on literacy, numeracy, and high school graduation, they encouraged schools to experiment by priming innovation with support and funding. The unwritten message was that schools and teachers needed to be key participants in improvement and that their ideas and knowledge mattered. This was a smart move early in the strategy, as it demonstrated trust in the profession, an essential ingredient for an effective partnership and buy-in from teachers. We see from the outset that the strategy kept a strong focus, shared responsibility through collaboration, and provided opportunity. It allowed teachers time to learn from one another and practice new ideas in nonthreatening situations.[29] In terms of our dynamic framework, there was a much better balance between push and pull actions.

While there was a common commitment to build partnerships with district school boards and teachers and to focus on improving teaching, the strategy used different tactics for elementary schools and for high schools, although in both cases strategies that focused on local capacity building and learning from implementation were prominent features. And there was a single coherent strategy with one set of expectations for teachers and students. At the outset in 2004 the Literacy and Numeracy Secretariat (LNS) was created to work with district school boards and elementary schools as a special purpose part of the ministry with more flexibility. It drew on expertise within the system and employed some of the best educators in Ontario as student achievement officers to work in partnership with district school boards. At the elementary level, literacy and math coaches were built into local budgets. The Student Success (SS) program for high schools took a different approach. The Liberal government initiated a "student success" strategy whereby each of the 900 secondary schools was funded to employ a Student Success Teacher (SST), whose job it was to work with school leadership and staff to help low-performing students. Each district school board was also funded to hire a Student Success Leader (SSL) to coordinate the work of SSTs. In the new strategy formulated in 2003–2004, ministry staff worked with SSLs individually and collectively to form a central team, share ideas, and implement the new policy on increasing high school graduation rates.

High School Reform

In 2003, high schools were still working through earlier reforms. The shift from a 5-year to a 4-year program culminated in a double cohort of students finishing high school in 2003 as the last of the 5-year graduates joined the first of those following the new 4-year program. The Ministry of Education commissioned a longitudinal study from 2000 to 2005 to evaluate the change from a 5-year to a 4-year program in terms of its impact on graduation rates.[30] With only 68% of students graduating in 2003, there was serious concern about the number of dropouts. A task group established the previous year to look at the problem posed by students at risk of dropping out reported to the education minister in January 2003.[31] Work continued despite the distractions of an election year, and *Building Pathways to Success* was published in October.[32]

In 2005 Alan King of Queen's University in Kingston, Ontario, rang alarm bells with the completed longitudinal study about the impact of the new 4-year high school program on graduation rates.[33] In order to graduate, a student needs to build up a total of 30 credits in high school. King reported that less than 16% of students who failed a credit in Grade 9 went on to graduate in 4 years. Furthermore, those who failed to accumulate credits at the required pace were on an ever-increasing risk of dropping out. Only 2 years into the Ontario Strategy, the government discovered that 27% of Grade 9 and 40% of Grade 10 students had failed at least one credit and were at risk of dropping out of high school.

This was the backdrop for the Student Success program of the new government that began by identifying the roots of the problem in high schools. Here we find a good balance across the second set of purposeful actions in our framework: using data from the King report to create a high sense of urgency, then adopting a problem-solving attitude to work out solutions with the people who would have to implement them. Working through the district school boards, the SS program provided resources and supported professional learning to develop literacy across the curriculum. It was committed to an 85% graduation rate by 2010. But the program had a broader goal than preventing dropouts; its components included:

- More focus on literacy and numeracy
- Effective transitions into and out of high schools
- Early identification of potential dropouts
- Increased student engagement
- Program innovations such as Specialist High Skills Majors (see below)
- Clearly demarcated pathways to postsecondary destinations

A committee of Student Success Leaders and education ministry staff developed a list of Student Success Indicators designed to provide early warnings of students who were likely to need additional support.[34] The SSTs in high schools kept track of at-risk students. Another report published in 2005 laid out these students' needs.[35] SSTs became student advocates, collaborating with parents and helping classroom teachers understand how they might adapt their teaching to match the particular needs of struggling students. The government's commitment was reinforced by legislation in

2005 that required all students who do not graduate to remain in some form of learning until they are 18 years old. Learning in this context includes college and workplace programs as well as high schools.

The government followed through by launching the Specialist High Skills Major (SHSM) program in 2006. SHSM allows students to focus on interests or talents they already have, develop specialist knowledge and skills, and earn credits and career-relevant qualifications while they continue to meet graduation requirements.[36] Schools were invited to submit proposals to develop a specialist program. It had to be related to significant industry or business employment opportunities near the school. The program started in fall 2006 with 600 students across the province following 44 individual programs in 27 (out of 800) high schools. By 2013, some 38,000 students were enrolled in 1,500 programs in 647 high schools. This is equivalent to 12% of the population in each grade.

Local Board Initiatives

When the new Ontario Strategy was initiated in 2003, some district school boards were several steps ahead of the government with effective working policies for literacy and numeracy; as a result, they became important resources for the province as a whole (e.g., by being released to work in the LNS, to spread capacity to other boards). From 2004–2006 the LNS asked all district school boards to show their most effective practices to support literacy and numeracy. They gathered information from 225 district-based practices that were often focused on school networking, collaboration, and job-embedded professional learning. That helped to kick-start the lateral capacity-building strategy. In 2006 the LNS published its first *Schools on the Move* report containing 23 case stories from elementary schools across the province that had significantly improved student outcomes from 2003 to 2005.[37] This launched the Lighthouse Program, intended to celebrate success and share good ideas by connecting these schools with others that had similar students but lower performance. Three more reports were published in later years showcasing work from 140 schools in the province. A similar report covering district school boards was published in 2006.[38] Using evidence from eight different boards, the report draws attention to successful district practices in four broad areas:

- Leading with purpose and focusing direction
- Designing a coherent strategy, coordinating implementation, and reviewing outcomes
- Developing precision in knowledge, skills, and daily practices for improving learning
- Sharing responsibility

A high school report dealt with effective district practices in literacy for grades 7–12 with contributions from 16 district school boards. These reports underscore the importance of engaging teachers and improving results by identifying and spreading effective practices from the ground up.[39] These are examples of the Ontario Strategy attracting and supporting schools in a process of continuous improvement. There has to be a balancing push as well. In the tri-level reform, that was the responsibility of the districts. And the picture, as always, was mixed. Some boards pushed these reports into their schools to motivate improvements; others didn't.

Peace and Stability

Midway through its first term, the government reached a landmark agreement with the teacher federations. In 2005 they signed a 4-year "peace and stability" pact. The federations supported the government's improvement strategy, and in return the government dealt with teachers' workload issues. They pledged funding for 5,000 new teaching jobs. These included art, languages, music, and PE specialists in elementary schools, and Student Success Teachers, already mentioned, in high schools. Class sizes were reduced in grades K–3 as part of the earlier commitment to 90% of classes at 20 or less, and elementary teachers were provided with more prep time in school.

Intervention

While test scores and graduation rates picked up overall from 2003, some schools didn't improve. In dealing with schools that were stuck, the Ontario Strategy sets itself apart from most jurisdictions in the United States and England by adopting a more balanced approach. In the United States under the NCLB legislation, schools that fail to make adequate yearly progress are publicly identified and given 3 years to improve. Continued failure triggers increasing sanctions leading to change in leadership and ultimately school closure or reconstitution. In many states, like New York, there is a separate regime of state sanctions in addition to those imposed by the federal NCLB. While these programs usually provide extra resources for schools, they also rely on primitive motivations of fear or survival. Perhaps the most damaging aspect is the public humiliation that teachers and students suffer.[40] Some people never recover from the psychological damage, and in England there are cases with direct links to suicide.

In the Ontario Tri-Level Reform Strategy, there is more dynamic symmetry between push and pull actions based on partnership rather than punishment. It built on the work of a turnaround program established before 2003. In 2006, recognizing that low-performing schools usually lack capacity rather than motivation (or as we might put it, persistent lack of success both reflects and causes low motivation), the government invested an annual C$25 million in the Ontario Focused Intervention Partnership (OFIP). This enabled the province, a district school board, and struggling elementary schools to work together and improve test scores. Overall, 1,100 elementary schools across all boards benefited from this additional investment in the first year. Another C$8 million provided preschool and after-school classes to help students catch up.[41] There was no shame attached to being in the program because it was recognized as a partnership issue. Attention was focused on capacity-building solutions to move ahead rather than looking back to make judgments and dish out blame. It was a differentiated program that picked up coasting schools as well as those that were obviously struggling. The three levels of schools needing support were:

1. Schools with less than 34% of students proficient at reading in 2 of the past 3 years
2. Schools with 34%–50% of students proficient at reading, but results were static or declining over the last 3 years
3. Schools with 51%–74% of students proficient at reading, but results were static or declining based on 3-year trends

What we learn most from this is that it is a fallacy that heavy-handed accountability will build success. Instead, the key to improving results is sharing accountability across the system.

External Evaluation

Two large-scale external evaluations were commissioned toward the end of the McGuinty government's first term in office. Both took several years to complete, and by the time the reports were published, the strategy was well into its second phase. In high schools, the Canadian Council on Learning concluded:

> Overall, the SS/L18 Strategy has garnered an enthusiastic response from all parties. While there are reservations about some features among some audiences, the dominant reaction is enthusiasm and optimism. Parents of students who have faced challenges report that their children have renewed interest in coming to school. Teachers and administrators who once looked forward to retirement have been reinvigorated and are planning to continue teaching. Students who endured their school experiences as they might a prison

sentence and students who have failed in school are experiencing success in opportunities that were previously unattainable.[42]

The evaluation of the elementary school reforms took longer, but in 2009 the Canadian Language and Literacy Research Network concluded:

Ontario's Literacy and Numeracy Secretariat has had a major, and primarily highly positive, impact on Ontario's education system. Overall, the level of activity associated with and generated by the LNS is very high. An impressive number of initiatives can be documented and broad support has been directed at the improvement of literacy and numeracy skills. Examples of the facilitative and direct roles that the LNS had played in helping to raise student achievement in Ontario have been described by boards, principals and individual teachers, as well as Ministry staff. A common message emerged from consideration of the work of the LNS in total: there has been a significant shift in the culture of Ontario schools that is focused on enabling the success of all students. There has also been sustained improvement in student achievement. These are major accomplishments. Most importantly, there have been clear, sustained and cumulative increases in the reading, writing and—to a lesser extent—mathematics achievement results of Ontario students, since the LNS began.[43]

Ontario Student Achievement, 2003–2007

EQAO test results are reported at four achievement levels, numbered 1 to 4. Level 3 is the proficiency level in each test, and Level 4 is higher than that. As we will shortly show, increased performance began immediately and set in over this initial 4-year period—we would say it was caused by a combination of focus, new resources, and mutual commitment between the government and schools (the latter all the more meaningful given the previous negative period). It should be noted that Level 3 is quite a high standard in two respects: first, the learning goals focus on critical thinking, communication, problem-solving, and other higher-order performance standards (in this sense they are comparable to the new Common Core State Standards in the United States); second, students must get a mark of 70% for a passing grade. Figures 3.2–3.4 show the percentages of students in each grade who achieved Levels 3 and 4 in the EQAO tests.

Test scores over the first term show improvements across the system, in all tests at all ages. These are impressive gains (math scores remain less impressive compared to literacy) following a period of stagnation prior to 2003. In most cases there is a leveling out from 2006 to 2007, and we see later how this develops during the government's second term. The strategy was clearly working, the class-size target was almost met, and

Figure 3.2. Proficiency Rates in EQAO Tests for Grade 3 Across Ontario from 2003–2007

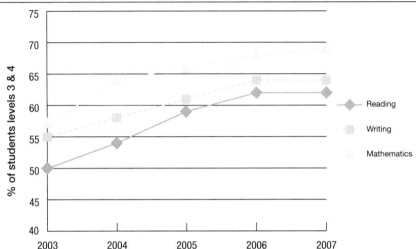

the system was on its way to meeting its other targets. The key to this success was getting a large number of leaders, or change agents, within and across schools, districts, and the province to jointly own the reform.[44] At this stage the reform relied on eight interdependent components:

- A guiding coalition (across three levels) constantly in communication
- Peace and stability, with no distracters
- LNS secretariat and SS team dedicated to the reforms
- Negotiating aspirational targets with districts and schools
- Capacity building in relation to those targets
- Growing the financial investment
- Evolving positive pressure within the system
- Connecting the dots with key complementary components (such as OFIP)

Ontario Strategy: Phase 2

As noted earlier, McGuinty was re-elected in October 2007. The second phase of the Ontario Strategy is described in *Energizing Ontario Education,* published in 2008.[45] The reforms picked up momentum in the second phase, and the sheer volume of work is enormous. We touch on the key features here, but we are conscious that while it does not tell the whole story, it is still a huge amount to assimilate in one reading. We suggest that

Figure 3.3. Proficiency Rates in EQAO Tests for Grade 6 Across Ontario from 2003–2007

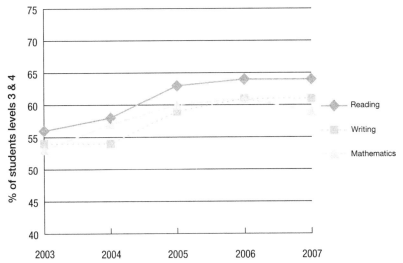

as you read through you keep the simple dynamic push and pull frame-work from Chapter 1 in your mind and use it to analyze the strategy. We draw attention to it in some places but not all.

Figure 3.4. Graduation and Proficiency Rates in EQAO Tests for Secondary Schools Across Ontario from 2003–2007

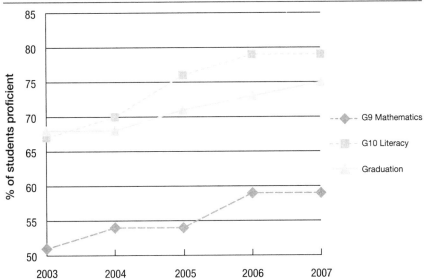

The strategy focused on a small number of clear commitments. Two were similar to earlier commitments, but this time the strategy replaced their class-size pledge with an equity goal:

1. High levels of student achievement
2. Reduced gaps in student achievement
3. Increased public confidence in publicly funded education

There were clearly shared targets for the tri-level reform. While the student achievement targets appeared the same, they were subtly modified making them realistic as well as aspirational:

- 75% of Grade 6 students reaching Levels 3 or 4. The drive to 75 continued, but no date was set for arrival (the first-term target date of 2008 had now passed). Instead, the policy emphasized the need to prepare students for a globalized economy in the 21st century by focusing on advanced literacy and numeracy skills.
- 85% of students graduating from high school. The target clarified achievement within 5 years of starting secondary school. Although high schools now had a 4-year program, the new target was working from the 2003 baseline of 68% graduating in 5 years.

The equity goal to close gaps in student achievement mentioned the following specific groups of students:

- Aboriginal (First Nation, Métis, and Inuit students)
- Recent immigrants
- Children from low-income families
- French-language students
- Boys
- Students with special needs

The document outlines some strategies to close the achievement gaps, including the Ontario Focused Intervention Partnerships explained earlier, but does not indicate by how much or by when this would be achieved. As a key goal, it indicates an awareness that these groups of students were underachieving and a strong commitment to respond.

While keeping its focus on three key commitments, the second-term strategy lists 11 supporting conditions that would contribute indirectly toward these goals:

- Early childhood learning
- Arts education

- Character development
- Student engagement
- Safe and healthy schools
- Parent engagement
- Peace and progress
- School-building repairs
- Small class sizes
- Professional learning
- Leadership

We now explore how some of these 11 conditions developed before turning to consider more direct work toward the three key goals. Not all of them are covered, and those that we deal with are in the same order as above.

A College of Early Childhood Educators was established for Ontario in 2007, the first of its kind in Canada. It is a self-regulatory body that registers everyone engaged in early childhood education, and sets and maintains professional standards. Charles Pascal was appointed as special adviser for early childhood learning. A major financial commitment was made by the government to fund full-day learning for all 4- and 5-year-olds (C$200 million in 2010 and C$300 million in 2011). Pascal produced a report about early learning in 2009.[46] A 5-year implementation plan was launched in 2010; by 2014, all elementary schools will offer free full-day kindergarten to all 4- and 5-year-olds. In 2012 the government, now in its third term, started consulting all concerned about a long-term vision for early learning and child care.[47] Wide-scale discussion led to the publication of a policy framework for a coordinated early-years system across the province.[48] In terms of our dynamic framework, this is another example of good balance between using data in Pascal's report to push forward plans and high investment in developing professional power in early childhood learning.

Most district school boards had already developed their own character development programs. The Ontario Strategy sought to find the common ground across them all and share ideas so that they might benefit from one another. This led to the publication of common beliefs and key principles to govern local programs across the province.[49] Work on student engagement was focused on adolescence and led to a unique document published by the ministry and endorsed by all four major teacher unions.[50] A new policy memorandum published in 2009 covered student discipline and positive behavior. Among other things, it provides a legal framework for developing school safety and includes a requirement for each school to complete a confidential student survey every 2 years.

The commitment to lateral capacity building continued, and some interesting work emerged from professional learning initiatives in the second term. A joint ministry and teacher federation task force created the Teacher Learning and Leadership Program (TLLP) for experienced teachers. It was reviewed by Ann Lieberman and later evaluated by Carol Campbell and Anna Yashkina.[51] Teachers made proposals for small grants (up to C$10,000) to fund their own professional learning projects directly linked to student learning. If selected, teachers had to commit to sharing the outcomes with others. Successful applicants received additional support from previous beneficiaries about wider dissemination of their work. Structured activities were developed for professional learning communities within schools.

Two student achievement officers in the LNS established the Teaching–Learning Critical Pathway (T-LCP).[52] Essentially, the T-LCP provides a model that helps teachers collaborate and gain deeper insights into their students' learning. Then in 2010 the LNS promoted Collaborative Inquiry as a new direction for professional learning as part of the capacity-building strategy.[53] This has strong similarities to Inquiry Teams developed in NYC (see Chapter 2). These are both examples of how student achievement officers from the Ministry of Education develop new ideas in partnership with teachers and leaders in districts, bring the ideas to the center, and then disseminate them across the province.

Leadership

In order to focus effort on the LNS and SS during the first phase, it was deliberately decided not to have a leadership strategy, although there was considerable work done to improve leadership. This was extended in the second phase with explicit work to increase leadership capacity. The Ontario Leadership Strategy was launched in 2008 with a 3-year implementation plan and a C$4 million annual budget.[54]

An internal evaluation led by Ken Leithwood from Ontario Institute for Studies in Education found that the strategy was particularly successful at working jointly across the system to improve learning and teaching in schools.[55] The leadership strategy developed an impressive range of resources for school and district leaders, including an Ontario Leadership Framework (OLF).[56] A companion to the leadership resources is the Ontario School Effectiveness Framework, developed by the LNS, which supports broader school improvement as well as leadership capacity.[57]

It is important to note that within the Ontario Ministry of Education there was a deliberate attempt to connect work more effectively across government departments. In the case of the leadership division, for example, it was clearly seen by that division that its mandate was to support the core priorities of literacy, math, and high school graduation.

Thus the leadership framework was intended to help districts develop their leadership capacity, short- and-long term, relative to the core reform agenda.

Ontario Student Achievement, 2007–2012

Next we consider work that was directly focused on the two achievement goals in the second term: raising standards and reducing gaps. As best practices were identified across the province, it was more efficient to focus on things that worked rather than reinvent wheels.[58] It was still lateral capacity building, since the ideas came from schools. The LNS supported critical literacy to help students acquire higher-order skills and deepen their understanding.[59]

In a review of the results of EQAO tests for Phase 2, the target was passed in writing at Grade 3, while reading improved more gradually after leveling out for a few years (see Figure 3.5). The most notable feature is hitting the literacy target in elementary schools with 75% of Grade 6 students achieving Level 3 or 4 in both reading and writing (see Figure 3.6). On the other hand, mathematics improved slightly and then declined.

Figure 3.5. Proficiency Rates in EQAO Tests for Grade 3 Across Ontario from 2007–2012

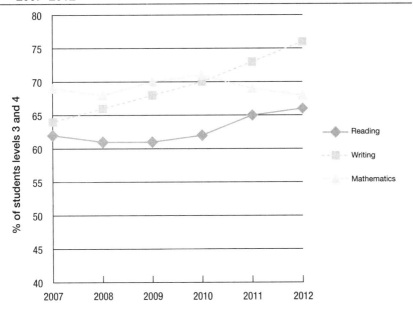

Figure 3.6. Proficiency Rates in EQAO Tests for Grade 6 Across Ontario from 2007–2012

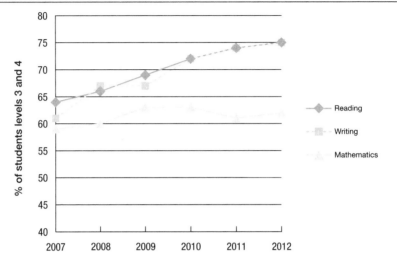

High schools continued to secure more effective learning for students at risk of not graduating. Dual-credit programs were developed and co-operative education expanded to complement the SHSM. Dual-credit programs allow students to follow approved apprenticeship or vocational college courses that will count as credits toward graduating from high school. Co-operative education allows students to earn credits by success-fully completing structured work placements.[60]

An audit of the Student Success initiatives was carried out by the Office of the Auditor General for Ontario in 2011.[61] This office is an independent agency that conducts value-for-money and financial audits of government ministries, services, and programs. The auditor noted steady progress toward the government goal of 85% graduation by 2011, pointing out commendable practice and areas for improvement.

Mathematics results in high schools at Grade 9 were much better (see Figure 3.7). They are the combined results for students following both the Academic and Applied tracks. Literacy at Grade 10 was flat through the second term, ending slightly lower. These are the results for students who pass the OSSLT in Grade 10; it does not include any who pass it later.

The key measure is the graduation rate, which increased steadily toward the 85% target. There was some debate about the graduation rate when the auditor drew attention to the fact that the percentage of students graduating in 4 years was lower (72% in 2010), but added that if the data were collected at age 25, then 91% graduated.[62] The target was always set as a 5-year graduation rate of 85%.

Figure 3.7. Graduation and Proficiency Rates in EQAO Tests for Secondary Schools Across Ontario from 2007–2012

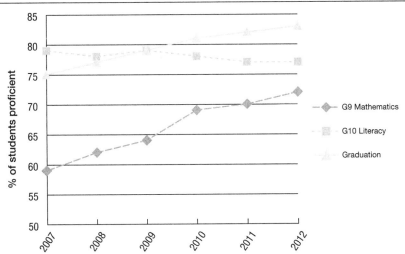

Reducing Gaps in Student Achievement

The ministry published a strategy for equity and inclusive education in 2009 together with a set of guidelines for implementation.[63] The guidelines indicate that district school boards are responsible for monitoring and reporting students' achievements so they can measure how they are reducing achievement gaps and inform everyone concerned. Some boards had already collected demographic data such as students' ethnicity and socioeconomic factors to be considered when planning to improve achievement. But this had not happened in all boards and still remains the case. Consequently, the province does not appear to have a systematic and coherent way to determine whether achievement gaps are being reduced for children from low-income homes or for different ethnic groups. The Auditor General touched on this issue in the 2011 annual report by pointing out that other successful jurisdictions target support to higher-risk groups of students based on ethnicity, disability, or economic status and have significantly reduced achievement gaps.[64] The report recommends that the ministry should "assess the viability of calculating student success indicators by a variety of attributes such as ethnicity, language and socioeconomic status."[65] Perhaps in this regard the Ontario Strategy is not pushy enough. There is a clear challenge to the status quo coming from the Auditor General to the ministry. As yet this remains unresolved.

In 2009 the Ontario Education Research Symposium chose the theme of closing achievement gaps.[66] Presentations and papers were grouped under five subthemes: students with special needs, English language learners, Aboriginal students, boys' literacy, and students in poverty. Here we review ministry activities related to these five subthemes. Later, we examine how they were developed by TDSB.

Students with Special Needs. An early change to funding for special education reduced paperwork in schools. A ministry task force for special educational needs, cochaired by Kathleen Wynne, was convened during the first term and reported in 2006.[67] Wynne became Minister of Education in the second term. The report recognized opposing views about inclusion of special education in mainstream classes and acknowledged that the preferred placement for all students should be the normal classroom, as far as possible.

An expert panel reported during the first term about teaching literacy and numeracy to students with special needs in grades K–6.[68] The ministry responded to this report in 2005 by granting C$25 million to the Council of Ontario Directors of Education (CODE) to develop and implement a plan that would support the recommendations from the expert panel. CODE designed and implemented a special education project called Essential for Some, Good for All (ESGA). It was a lateral capacity-building program to enhance teachers' professional learning and increase achievement of those students with special educational needs. In 2009 CODE engaged Andy Hargreaves and his team from Boston College to review ESGA.[69] Their report draws attention to the different approach used by ESGA to change teachers' practice and compares it favorably to the more traditional, top-down, centralized, data-driven strategies that often rely on market forces as they encourage competition between schools, and to bottom-up methods that lack coherence. Hargreaves and his team called the strategy "Leadership from the Middle" (i.e., the district layer of tri-level reform), in which district leadership as a collective entity (CODE) takes responsibility for developing the strategy for the system. Such a strategy combines pressure and support in a more natural manner, built into the action of peers that focus on new improvements. Here we have another external evaluation that recognizes the value of balanced purposeful actions in terms of push and pull dynamics.

Early in the second term the Auditor General carried out an audit of special education. The audit noted that schools did not measure the achievement gap between students with special needs and regular curriculum expectations. Consequently, they were unable to judge whether any change in the performance gap was appropriate in the circumstances.[70] In 2011 the ministry published a guide for the effective assessment and instruction for all students. It includes a section on understanding achievement gaps and how to close them.[71]

We analyzed gaps between students with special educational needs and those without in EQAO tests from 2003 to 2012. (Detailed analysis is available in online Appendix B at www.tcpress.com). The gap was reduced in literacy at Grade 6 and writing at Grade 3. In other tests the gaps between students with special needs and all other students have not been reduced; in fact, the gap has widened in mathematics at Grades 3 and 6 as well as in the Grade 10 literacy test.

English Language Learners. In 2006 about 20% of students tested at Grade 3 were described as English language learners.[72] A practical guide to help teachers working with English language learners in their classrooms was published in 2005.[73] At the start of the second term, the ministry followed this with a policy framework and guidelines covering K–12.[74] In the policy the government gives a broad description of English language learners. They include Canada-born Aboriginal students as well as others who prefer a distinct cultural identity and do not speak English at home or in their close community. It also includes recently arrived immigrants who speak languages other than English. The policy promotes a consistent approach while allowing district school boards flexibility. The purpose is to help these students quickly gain sufficient fluency in English so they can be successful in school. More detailed guidance for particular age groups was published subsequently.[75]

We analyzed gaps between English language learners and the rest in EQAO tests from 2003 to 2012. (Detailed analysis is available in online Appendix B at www.tcpress.com). The general trend in these results shows that the achievement gap between English language learners and all other students has been halved in a decade.

Aboriginal Students. The specific needs of First Nation, Métis, and Inuit students fall within the general category of Aboriginal students. In 2007 it was estimated that over 50,000 Aboriginal students attended public elementary and high schools in Ontario. More than half of them lived in Toronto. A new policy framework published in the same year included a strategic plan linked to the three government education goals with specific performance indicators.[76] The plan discussed the difficulty of measuring Aboriginal student achievement, while the performance data do not identify them. It proposed that district school boards should consult with their communities about confidential self-identification by Aboriginal students.[77] There is some dispute about the validity of EQAO tests for Aboriginal students. Lorenzo Cherubini, Director of the Tecumseh Centre for Aboriginal Research at Brock University, argues that the cultural bias in EQAO tests makes them invalid as a measure to assess the achievement of Aboriginal students.[78] A separate ministry document gave more advice to boards about how they might proceed.[79] The policy was backed with C$22.7 million, and activities included employing more Aboriginal staff in schools, training teachers, creating new resources, and working with parents.

In 2012 the Auditor General used census data to report that 66% of Aboriginal young adults between ages 20 and 24 graduated from high school in 2006 compared with 89% of all Ontarians, a gap of 23 percentage points.[80] The purpose of the audit was to assess whether the ministry and school boards had adequate procedures in place to improve achievement of Aboriginal students and ensure that the money allocated was spent on appropriate initiatives. Five years after the publication of the policy, less than half of the estimated Aboriginal population had self-identified.[81] Of those Aboriginal students who had self-identified in 2012, only 45% at Grade 10 were on track to graduate compared with 74% for all Grade 10, a gap of 29 percentage points.[82] While this is a partial measure and therefore unreliable, it suggests that the goal of reducing achievement gaps for Aboriginal students has not yet been achieved across the province. This is a sensitive issue where being too pushy may cause irreparable damage. It is difficult to get the balance right and remains a work in progress.

Boys' Literacy. A teacher inquiry project into boys' literacy was carried out from 2005 to 2008, paid for by the ministry and led by the Ontario Institute for Studies in Education. A final report was published in 2009.[83] This collaborative project worked in both elementary schools and high schools. The report includes qualitative data about improved boys' attitudes and 10 broad areas of impact.

Students in Poverty. As with Aboriginal students, the province does not separate test and graduation results for children in poverty even though SES is known to be the most powerful single influence on student outcomes. Consequently, there is no benchmark or way of knowing whether any achievement gaps for these students have been reduced. An indirect focus came through schools supported by the Ontario Focused Intervention Partnership. A 2010 report about OFIP shows that the schools in the partnership tended to have higher proportions of students from low-income families.[84] And the community-based organization People for Education reports that schools with low average family incomes have greater access to family-support programs and full-day kindergarten.[85]

Summary of the Ontario Education Strategy

We have described how the tri-level reform in Ontario developed over the last decade. Before moving on to examine how TDSB engaged with it, we first summarize the strategy under its three key features:

Progressive Partnership

- Guiding coalition formed among all three levels (province, district, school)
- Authentic trust and engagement among the levels
- Shared expectations for and from each level
- Clear roles and responsibilities for each level

Resolute Focus

- Small number of ambitious goals
- Clear, easy to understand goals, acceptable to everyone
- Stuck with goals to the end, didn't get sidetracked or overloaded
- Focus on data as an instrument of continuous improvement
- Peace and stability

Collaborative Capacity Building

- Not top-down or bottom-up
- Inquiry-based approach, learning as we go
- Resources focused for maximum leverage
- Schools spreading good practice among themselves
- Nonpunitive intervention for schools in need

Simple things are often difficult to achieve and even more difficult to keep in balance. The original peace and stability pact between the government and the teacher federations expired in August 2008. It was replaced by another 4-year collective agreement that ran out in 2012. Premier McGuinty was then into his third term of office. In the 2011 election the Liberals failed to win an overall majority but were still the largest party with one parliamentary seat less than the combined Conservative and NDP members. Contract negotiations with teacher federations began in February 2012 in an austere financial climate and failed to reach agreement. With the support of Conservatives, the Liberals passed the Putting Students First Act (Bill 115), which withdrew teachers' bargaining rights, made strikes illegal, cut their sick-day allowance, and imposed a pay freeze. Teachers responded by stopping all extracurricular activities and staging walkouts during the fall. In October 2012 McGuinty announced his intention to step down from the premiership as soon as his party had chosen a new leader. In January 2013 former education minister Kathleen Wynne was selected by the Liberal party to be the new premier of Ontario. In the first six months of 2013 Premier Wynne re-established collective agreements with all teacher unions. Since the current contract runs only to August 2014, it is not clear what will happen beyond that. One of Premier

McGuinty's last acts was to request a paper from Michael Fullan about the next stage of reform. This paper, titled *Great to Excellent,* captures the accomplishments of the 2003 to 2012 period, and serves as the ongoing policy strategy in Ontario at the present time.[86]

As we leave the Ontario Strategy we note how important it turned out to be for the Toronto District and for other school districts that a relatively effective provincewide strategy was in place, since districts benefit or suffer depending on the province policy context and actions. Perhaps this is a topic for another time.

TORONTO DISTRICT SCHOOL BOARD

We have called the Toronto decade "Success Amidst the Rocks" because the district had a tradition of operating with a degree of conflict and turmoil at the top (among the board of trustees, with the government), while at the same time having the capacity to carry out some very effective improvement strategies. The work of the district became more complicated when amalgamation occurred in 1998, integrating seven previous boards into one megaboard—the Toronto District School Board (TDSB). What is remarkable about the Toronto case is that a strong seam of instructional improvement linked to student achievement grew and became increasingly strong during the 2003–2013 decade.

We begin by considering some of the tensions between the Toronto District School Board and the Ontario Ministry of Education that contributed to a slow start for the reforms in Toronto. We describe in more detail the features of the Ontario reforms that had the greatest impact on student achievement in Toronto. In doing so, we see how they were successfully implemented. We also include other initiatives promoted by TDSB that are not part of the Ontario Strategy but have improved students' achievements. Finally, we compare student test scores in Toronto with the overall average for Ontario.

Overcoming Inertia

Toronto District School Board is by far the largest and most complex district in Ontario. TDSB, as noted, was formed in 1998 by merging the seven urban school boards of Metropolitan Toronto. Each of these legacy boards had administered its schools for many years. There were dominant cultures—traditions that have not yet faded, even after 16 years trying to create alignment and coherence through a commonly owned strategy. In the new board, schools are arranged in families of schools loosely based on ward boundaries (TDSB has 22 elected trustees from 11 wards). Each family of schools has a mix of 25–30 elementary and high schools, led by an area superintendent. Initially there were 24 families of schools across the district, although this has been restructured with falling rolls to 20. Each TDSB family of schools is larger than some school boards elsewhere in Ontario. The families of schools enjoy high levels of professional autonomy led by the superintendents with the close involvement of trustees. This independence, coupled with less direct connection from the center to the schools in a larger organization, meant that the Ontario reforms were slower to gain traction in TDSB compared with most other school boards across the province.

The synchronization of staff, policies, procedures, and finances across an organization of this size needed time and stability to work through the system, which employed 17,000 teachers and 9,000 support staff in 591 schools and educated 272,000 students.[87] We have already described the turbulence in the overall system when the TDSB was created. The provincial government had removed the powers that district school boards had to levy their own taxes. The former Toronto Board of Education, the largest board of those amalgamated, had financed itself almost completely from local taxes with very little reliance on provincial funds and thus saw itself as largely independent from the province. TDSB was forced to work with the budget allocated by the Ontario Ministry of Education. The government expected efficiency savings in line with its reduced public spending to provide tax breaks. Because TDSB's allocation, based on average costs across the province, failed to take account of the real costs of education in an urban setting, TDSB was unable to set a balanced budget. Trustees on TDSB were divided between those who opposed cuts to services and those who favored compliance with the government-imposed financial limit. This division was split according to the legacy boards. The former Toronto Board of Education, which had a track record of supporting more progressive and diverse programs, opposed the cuts.[88] The situation was further aggravated in 2001 by the departure of the first director (chief superintendent) of the TDSB, Marguerite Jackson, who was in the post for only 3 years. In 2002 the provincial government intervened, removed the budget from TDSB's control, and installed a supervisor to enforce undertakings within the fiscal curb.

At the start of the Ontario reforms in 2003, relations between TDSB and the Ontario Ministry of Education suffered from a hangover of suspicion. Coherence remained a challenge within TDSB, which operated as 24 autonomous families of schools. For example, school improvement planning was well established in some families of schools but not in others. Some superintendents were overwhelmed by discipline issues and operational functions; they had little time for instructional leadership. An added dimension was the attitude of some trustees. The board had a reputation for being cantankerous at best, while others describe trustees as disrespectful to staff, referring to video evidence from board meetings that may be viewed online.[89] TDSB's second director, David Reid, was appointed in 2002 and also lasted 3 years. His departure was linked to strained relationships with trustees and parents.[90] He was replaced by Gerry Connelly in 2005 as interim director. Connelly was approaching retirement in 2008 but agreed to stay on until the board appointed a new director. It took the trustees more than a year to recruit Chris Spence in 2009. Spence was a charismatic leader who resigned in 2013 after he admitted plagiarism in an article he wrote for the *Toronto Star* newspaper.[91]

It would be difficult to create more unfavorable conditions at the top than these while implementing the Ontario reforms using a tri-level strategy built around stability and professional harmony among the ministry, the district, and the schools. Despite this turmoil at the top, TDSB had a number of good instructional leaders at the second level down (deputy directors), among the 24 area superintendents, and among school principals and teacher leaders. The new work of implementation was furthered with the appointment in 2013 of Donna Quan as interim director, and then affirmed as official director shortly thereafter; Quan was one of the key instructional leaders at the deputy director level working across the system.

A key theme in the TDSB case is how a seam of commitment to instructional improvement and student achievement can survive and in fact thrive under very difficult conditions of constant disruption. Early in the amalgamation period, TDSB undertook a consultative process that resulted in the endorsement of three key priorities: closing the achievement gap, engaging parents and communities, and ensuring financial stability. While the third priority has not had a smooth ride, the first two have enjoyed remarkable (considering the conditions) vitality. We attribute this to a combination of endorsed priorities, specific strategies, and the commitment of key leaders on the senior team—such as Director Donna Quan and associate directors who were able to maintain a focus on student learning amid the distractions. In spite of the ongoing tensions, the work on school improvement and student achievement remained a core priority. For example, TDSB is one of the leading boards in the province in using data to measure outcomes and inform decisions and instructional practices. From the outset the district established its own Office of Accountability and Student Achievement, headed by an executive who reported directly to the director.

Another key initiative that illustrated TDSB's leadership and commitment to increased student achievement was the innovative Early Years Literacy Project (EYLP), and the corresponding Early Years Numeracy

Project (EYNP). Literacy and math leaders and coaches were provided to the 24 area superintendents as part of their resources teams to work alongside teachers as an "external-internal" expertise resource—which was established even before the provincial Literacy and Numeracy Secreatariat. These two initiatives contributed to successes in improving learning in schools through the introduction of systemwide diagnostic assessments undertaken by all K–8 teachers twice a year, resulting in developing teacher competencies in diagnosing learning in order to design learning tasks that are curriculum based.

In some ways, then, TDSB was out in front of the province in 2003, when the overall system strategy commenced. After a slow start with respect to connecting province and TDSB forces, the two systems began to link more directly. The Ontario Focused Intervention Partnership (OFIP), which focused on lower-performing and stagnant schools, is a good case in point. When OFIP started, TDSB had 150 schools so designated; today that number has been reduced to 10. Similarly, the province's powerful High Skills Majors initiative has been increasingly adopted by TDSB.

Finally, TDSB has been an innovative force in forging the connection between equity and excellence. Over the decade, leadership has defined its moral imperative as addressing the opportunity and participation gaps of subgroups. For example, the Model Schools for Inner Cities (MCIS) initiative, established in 2006 with three pilot schools, has grown rapidly to over 150 schools. Comprehensive solutions to equity and excellence focusing on student achievement and well-being and parent and community engagement are developed, assessed, and spread (oursite.tdsb.on.ca/org/MSIC).

The lesson is that a core, relentless commitment to the student achievement agenda can be successfully pursued, even under rocky conditions, and that this commitment has a life of its own, independent of the province strategy, while at the same time being able to join up with converging external strategies. There is still much more to be done in this mega-city school district, but we will see that growth is possible, even under arid conditions and diversions.

Implementation

There is a consensus among the leaders of both the district and the ministry that the following features had the most impact on the improved standards in TDSB:

- Relentlessly focused resources devoted to equity and excellence
- Appropriate intervention
- District reviews
- Improvement planning

- Capacity building
- Leadership development
- Continued pursuit of equity

Relentlessly Focused Resources

Despite the slow start in TDSB (although as we noted there was a strong seam of activity related to equity and student achievement that pre-dated the Ontario Strategy), the reforms picked up pace by 2010. The focus on a few key goals in terms of higher expectations of students' achievements made a big difference. The alignment of data was important, coupled with the growth of skills and ability to compare and manipulate the data. TDSB had an edge in this respect with a well-established and re-spected research department that supported the system with data analysis and professional development. The department provides contextualized data for schools so that they can compare their progress with other schools that have a similar profile. The intense focus on higher expectations with accountability led to more precise conversations between district and school leaders about which students needed most support and how it was going to be provided. Then it was the resources, human and financial, that came with the Ontario Strategy that made the difference. Today the district and the schools feel that they are part of a larger plan. There is a sense that they are all in this together. Nobody comes to the table thinking that he or she has all the answers. There is a shared vision that the ministry has resourced and that the system has been implementing. This process of implementation is more consistent at the elementary school level than in the high schools, but there are several examples of high schools that have also progressed relative to the Ontario Strategy. Once again we find the balance between challenging the status quo and developing a com-monly owned strategy. Don't let the simplicity fool you; this was difficult to achieve in a district that was reluctant to engage or, one could say, that had other distractions drawing its attention. It relied heavily on the pro-fessional skills, patience, and persistence of key leaders on both sides—in the LNS and TDSB.

The size of TDSB made it less responsive in terms of high school re-forms. As explained earlier, each district was funded to appoint one School Success Leader, whose influence varied with the number of schools. In a small district, the SSL deals personally with all of its high schools. In TDSB the SSL is not able to have the same personal engagement with 105 high schools. Although TDSB was able to appoint a second tier of senior prin-cipals and a third tier of teacher leaders, they could not have the same de-gree of influence as an SSL in a smaller district. Added to that, in TDSB the SSL had other responsibilities in addition to the Ontario Strategy. Another factor was opposition posed by some trustees who determine policy in the district. Implementation of the Specialists High Skills Majors (SHSM), which has made a significant impact on graduation rates across the province, was stalled by trustees in TDSB.[92] As reported earlier, across Ontario 38,000 students were enrolled in SHSM programs in 2013. Students in TDSB make up 12.7% of the students in the province, so an even distribution would place 4,800 TDSB students in a specialist program. The total was actually 1,700. This partly explains the widening gap between TDSB and Ontario graduation rates (shown in Figure 3.10 later in this chapter).

Appropriate Intervention

The Ontario Focused Intervention Partnership was an early part of the Ontario Strategy in 2003, and we described it earlier in this chapter. The program relied on trust between all concerned, and that was not always the case at first. The LNS surveyed teachers before and after OFIP. Before intervention, more teachers blamed external factors such as poverty roughly 2:1. After OFIP, the opinions shifted to 1:2, with more teachers admitting they could do something about it. Across the province the OFIP strategy was a big success. Combining high expectations, nonjudgmental (positive) stances toward the schools, and targeted and ongoing support for capacity building, the strategy worked to reduce the number of low-performing schools from an initial group of some 800 schools to 87 schools. In TDSB 150 schools in OFIP were reduced to 10. This was accomplished through a combination of the involvement of superintendents, a shift from professional development to professional learning, more sophisticated use of data, and a deliberate focus on improving teaching.

In TDSB everyone kept hearing that OFIP schools were using "moderated marking" and it was making a real difference. Lots of other schools started wondering what moderated marking was and visiting OFIP schools to learn more about it. The good practice was beginning to spread around the district. Using assessment data has been a significant feature of the improvement strategy. As the strategy progressed, the data became more precise. TDSB was able to use its families of schools data and statistical neighbors to raise expectations. Closing schools or labeling them as failing was not part of the Ontario intervention strategy. There was never a sense that you might lose your job if you missed a target. The partnership approach, engaging ministry, district, and school staff, was always, "This is one of our schools. How can we work together and help to improve it?"

A similar approach has been developed with high schools. The lowest-performing third of high schools across the province are following the Student Success School Support Initiative (SSSSI) led by the Ministry of Education. TDSB was already working under its own initiative with 25 schools on its Urban Diversity Strategy since 2008. Additional funding from the ministry through the SSSSI project enabled TDSB to extend the work to 41 schools. These are schools with higher proportions of students who are struggling to succeed. Intervention in high schools is more challenging, given their greater autonomy and internal departmental structures. The current approach uses collaborative inquiry with teams of teachers, including the principal, working together to analyze student data with more precision and developing strategies that will first move the students and later move the school toward higher performances. The involvement of the principal in these teams is essential. It reinforces the need for essential instructional leadership in schools with low performance. As we noted earlier, any intervention is a pushy action in our dynamic framework. If intervention is an important part of system-level improvement, as it was here in TDSB, then it must be balanced by equally purposeful pulling actions such as those described above.

District Reviews

Donna Quan, Director of Education at TDSB, has evidence showing that District Reviews of schools have made the biggest impact on student achievement in recent years. In 2007 the LNS published its first School Effectiveness Framework (SEF) for elementary schools. Following extensive feedback, the Ministry of Education released a draft K–12 framework in 2009 for consultation and then a complete SEF for both elementary and high schools in 2010. The SEF is a tool for school self-assessment and improvement planning. Student achievement is at the heart of the SEF and it is geared to raising standards. The same framework forms the basis of the District Review process. The process involves an external team of reviewers from the district who help the school monitor its progress. It has three stages:

1. Agreement between the school and the District Review team about the scope of the review. This builds on the school's self-assessment and how far it has implemented its improvement plans.
2. Site visit by the District Review team to collect evidence from conversations with staff and students, observations of students and staff at work in classrooms, and a scrutiny of students' work. The District Review team analyzes the evidence collected and prepares feedback.
3. Feedback to school staff in both conversation and written forms. Feedback covers general observations related to

students' learning, as well as noting areas of strength in terms of improvement. The team refers to degrees of consistency they observed between different grades, divisions, or departments in the school and makes suggestions about next steps.

Successful District Reviews rely on collaborative and respectful inter-actions between school staff and the District Review team. Communica-tion is open, honest, and transparent throughout the process. The District Review team adopts a supportive and nonjudgmental approach.

As with other Ontario strategies, District Reviews were implemented at a different pace in each district. In this regard TDSB was more active than some other boards, particularly with high school District Reviews. TDSB was successful at dealing with this contentious issue because they approached the labor groups first and had teacher and principal repre-sentatives around the table to design the procedures. In the first couple of years they were feeling their way and allowed some messy, on-the-go conversations to develop. Once it was established, the conversations be-came more focused, precise, and helpful. District Reviews have drawn superintendents and district instructional leaders into classrooms to look closely at students' learning and see firsthand what opportunities exist for further development. Current conversations focus on the differences between a good and a great school. All of these forces are pushing schools in a positive direction: a great example of systemwide improvement that penetrates the system to reach what really matters most—classroom in-struction. TDSB moved further than other districts because it had a bal-anced approach, keeping the pushy nature of the process but pulling people into its design.

While the main priority for each District Review is to help the school under review to move forward, the accumulation of qualitative evidence from across schools also helps to shape district improvement plans. TDSB has taken this a step further and used District Reviews to follow general themes across the district, such as structured learning in early-years set-tings and how inclusion is working for learners with special educational needs. In 2012 TDSB completed over 100 District Reviews and the pro-cess continued through labor disputes. It was well on track to review all schools over a 3-year cycle.

Improvement Planning

School improvement planning was consistent across TDSB after 2010. Before that, some families of schools had been using their own planning frameworks for many years, depending on the superintendent. It involved around 60% of the schools, although the practice varied. In some schools the whole staff was engaged in self-assessment and determined school priorities. In other schools it was confined to the principal and superintendent and the conversations were more guarded, depending on what resources might be available. Making it mandatory across the district has increased accountability, made the improvement process more explicit, and engaged the whole community. It is an essential part of the District Reviews.

Around the same time, the ministry required all district school boards to submit a Board Improvement Plan for Student Achievement (BIPSA). This is now well established and is the focus of dialogue between ministry and district leaders on three visits across each school year. BIPSA uses a framework with four areas for improvement across the province:

- Literacy
- Numeracy
- Learning pathways
- Community, culture, and caring

Schools in TDSB use the same four areas as a framework for school improvement planning, and the Board Improvement Plan is attached to each School Improvement Plan. There are direct links in each school improvement plan, drawn from their self-assessment, to school targets that are aligned with TDSB collective goals and the provincial priorities. The whole planning process has enabled TDSB to set very ambitious goals, such as a 10% increase in reading grades by a specified date.

Capacity Building

Improving the skills of teachers and leaders across any system is an essential part of raising student achievement. A recent report from TDSB draws attention to the success that blended professional learning (a mix of face-to-face and online learning) has in terms of changing instruction.[93] A significant feature of the Ontario Strategy has been the movement of leaders from districts to work in the ministry for a while before moving back to their district. It enables a cross-fertilization of ideas and a broadening of vision for both the ministry and the individuals concerned. While in the ministry, the opportunity to work in different districts and broaden experience leads ultimately to a deeper understanding, which is then taken back to the home district when the individual returns. Working relationships between colleagues that are established while they work at the ministry also support ongoing collaboration between districts for their mutual benefit. At any one time there may be 20 people from TDSB working in different capacities for the ministry. Within TDSB there is a similar movement, with teachers coming from their individual schools to work on curriculum across schools and then moving back into their own school. This two-way flow between ministry and district (in this case TDSB) personnel is a powerful latent strategy for building relationships, knowledge, capacity, and trust between the government and the district.

As part and parcel of the focus on instruction, the Ontario Strategy involved shifting from formal professional development events to supporting ongoing learning in schools. Sometimes referred to as "learning is the work," the change has been from professional development in workshops led by experts to professional learning in schools. The Teaching–Learning Critical Pathways was articulated by the LNS in its Capacity Building series of short publications in 2008 and in *Collaborative Inquiry*, published in 2010.[94] These developments encouraged teachers to work together in their own school, focus on marginalized students, and use more precise data analysis to move the students on. Through moderated marking and coteaching, this form of professional learning has also moved schools on. Some refer to it as the deprivatization of the classroom, and it did not happen until the Ontario Strategy was well on its way. It is the early days for this kind of work in high schools, where it still has a long way to go.

This shift to day-to-day capacity building was not mandated or part of a deliberate strategy. It spread like a virus rather than through any form of cascade or structured dissemination. TDSB engaged with this form of professional learning in a big way. Some superintendents pushed it with all the schools in their family. They were able to draw on extra resources from the ministry for release time that enabled teachers to work together. It was a big breakthrough for the Ontario Strategy in TDSB. This was most evident in high schools where previously it had been very difficult to make headway with instructional leadership. In the 41 schools working with the SSSSI, the program insists that the principal must be involved in the collaborative inquiry. It is not acceptable to delegate to the department head. This raises the status of the work, makes it more likely that it will eventually move the whole school forward, and demonstrates the importance of instructional leadership as the principal's main priority. Here again, we have examples of a dynamic balance of pushing and pulling actions between the ministry and the district and between superintendents and their schools.

Leadership Development

TDSB launched its own Learning and Leadership Academy in 2011 that builds on the success of the Ontario Leadership Strategy. The TDSB academy is a support program rather than a site. It includes leadership development across multiple pathways for aspiring leaders, teacher leaders, vice principals, and principals. The academy covers mentoring, shadowing, internships, and induction. It applies to business staff as well as those directly involved with instruction. It challenges support staff not only for their operational role but also for how they may contribute to student achievement.

Pursuing Equity

The legacy boards from which TDSB was formed all had explicit policies to promote greater equity in schools. Since its formation, TDSB has led the province with its commitment to many equity issues. The TDSB Equity Foundation Statement published in 2000 formed the basis of the provincial guidelines for inclusive schools published in 2009.[95] This statement expresses the board's commitment to pursue greater equity for students in terms of their ethnicity, gender, sexual orientation, poverty, and disability. Each of these commitments was followed by explicit actions. In 2011 TDSB published its Opportunity Gap Action Plan. This document sets out the planned work related to equity and inclusion over 4 years. It was the first time that all this work had been set out in one coherent plan; previously, it was more piecemeal. The plan is based on a rigorous analysis of TDSB students' test results and data gathered from its student and parent census.

TDSB was the first district in Ontario to survey students, in 2006, and also their parents, in 2008, about learning and life in and out of school. The surveys were repeated in 2011 and 2012. The response rate was extremely high, with 103,000 (90%) high school students completing the survey and 90,000 (two-thirds) responses from parents with children in elementary schools. These data were then matched with achievement data, and a series of census portraits was published.[96] They provide rich information to inform school and board improvement plans.

An example of effective action is Focus on Youth Toronto (FOYT). Nonprofit organizations are offered free use of TDSB school space for organized activities on the condition that they provide employment and leadership opportunities for young people from these communities. TDSB set a hiring target of between 350 and 400 FOYT youth workers for its seventh summer program in 2013. FOYT youth workers have been tracked and show increased achievement and well-being after this program.

The most ambitious and far-reaching program devised by TDSB in pursuit of greater equity is Model Schools for Inner Cities (MSIC), which we referenced earlier. Over 150 elementary and high schools with the largest concentration of families below the poverty line are supported by the

MSIC program.[97] These are the schools that require the most support to close achievement gaps for their students. The program was launched in 2006 with just three schools, and it has grown rapidly on the heels of its success. The 157 schools are grouped in seven elementary clusters and one secondary cluster. Each cluster employs a lead teacher, two teaching and learning coaches, three community support workers, and a coordinating principal. These staff help schools bring the essential components of MSIC to life.

Toronto Student Achievement, 2002–2012

About 20% of students in Ontario are taught in TDSB schools. Consequently, trends across TDSB results will inevitably show up in the Ontario averages. Demographic data about the population of Toronto show that it is not typical of Ontario overall. Like other big cities, Toronto is home to the very rich and the very poor, with higher proportions of families on low incomes than the rest of Ontario. We see in Figures 3.8 and 3.9 that there is no separation at Grades 3 and 6 between the Ontario and TDSB averages.

There is a difference in high schools, shown in Figure 3.10. Improvements in Grade 9 mathematics and Grade 10 literacy are at a higher rate in Toronto than in the rest of the province. TDSB was 9 percentage points in mathematics and 11 in literacy below the Ontario average in 2003. Those gaps drop to 1 and 3 percentage points respectively in 2012. The graduation rate is more interesting. In 2005 there was not much difference and it closed to 1 percentage point in 2006. Since then the improvements in TDSB have lagged slightly behind Ontario's steady increases. There is a 3 percentage point gap in 2012. We speculate that this may be connected to the slower adoption of the SHSM program in Toronto than in the rest of the province. In any case, high school graduation rates across the TDSB's 105 schools—many operating in very difficult circumstances, with the same challenges as big-city high schools in NYC and London—have moved steadily upward from 69% in 2005 to 80% in 2012.

We analyzed gaps for students with and without special needs and for English language learners and all other students over the decade in EQAO tests. (A detailed analysis is available in online Appendix B at www.tcpress.com). There are similar trends at Grades 3 and 6 in TDSB and Ontario (see above) apart from the gaps for English language learners. Gaps for these students in Grade 3 across Ontario have been more than halved, whereas in Toronto they have closed, then opened again by 2012. Similarly, in Grade 6, achievement gaps for English language learners across Ontario have been significantly reduced, while in Toronto the gaps in reading and writing are much wider.

Figure 3.8. Percentage of Grade 3 Students at Levels 3 and 4 in EQAO Tests for Reading, Writing, and Mathematics in Toronto and Ontario

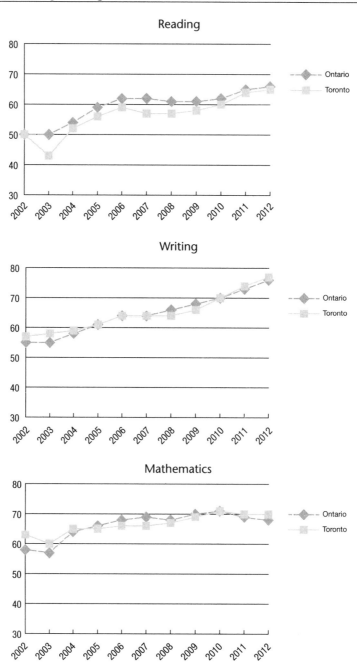

Figure 3.9. Percentage of Grade 6 Students at Levels 3 and 4 in EQAO Tests for Reading, Writing, and Mathematics in Toronto and Ontario

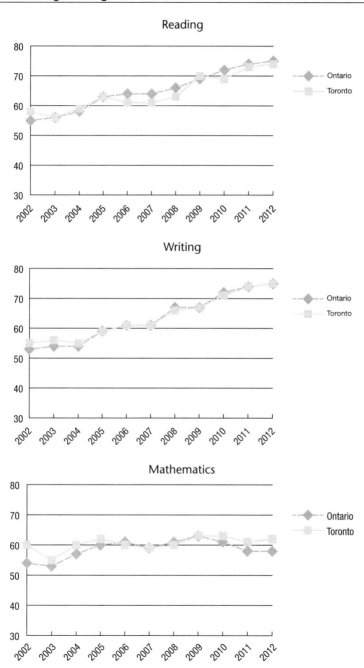

Figure 3.10. Percentage of Students at Levels 3 & 4 in Grade 9 Mathematics (Academic & Applied Combined); Passing OSSLT in Grade 10; and Graduating After 5 Years of High School in Toronto and Ontario

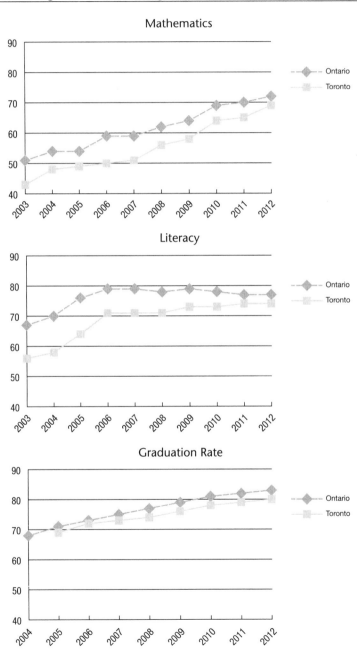

CONCLUSION: SUCCESS AMIDST THE ROCKS

We take up the cross-case lessons among the three big-city cases in Chapter 5. The Toronto case is very instructive. Here we have a district with all the problems of a big city, including a degree of instability of top leadership and a history of amalgamating seven previous cultures and a group of 22 trustees, many of whom operated in their own wards or were otherwise fragmented when it came to overall policy. One can only imagine the constant policy demands and distractions with all the complexities of an urban agenda, and a board of 22 active trustees operating in a wardlike fashion. Yet TDSB was remarkably successful in relation to the bottom line of instructional improvements and corresponding student achievement. Somehow a critical mass of leaders at the next level down was able to maintain a focus on instruction.

To us this came about for several interrelated reasons. First, TDSB had a built-in commitment to excellence and equity, along with specific mechanisms and strategies focusing on student achievement that preceded the province's strategy. Second, the province had a clear, intrusive, but helpful focus, along with resources and capacity building, which eventually converged in the same direction as the district strategy. There are scores of teachers, school, and district leaders who are attracted to the moral imperative agenda, especially when there are strategies to help realize it. Finally, although local politics and governance served up constant distractions, unlike New York City these issues did not intrude directly into the teaching and learning domain. There is a lesson there that we will pick up in the final chapter.

CHAPTER 4

London

Success Against the Odds

London, England, is an interesting case study because of its complexity and presence of incredibly difficult urban conditions for reform. Against almost all odds, two of its boroughs became highly successful, and an overall strategy, the London Challenge, made significant contributions. We should also say at the outset that unlike the New York case, the London case (and the Toronto case in Chapter 3) occurred in the context of a state-level strategy that focused on comprehensive implementation of a small number of ambitious goals. These strategies constituted an explicit external framework of push–pull forces that affected the cities—mostly for the better, we would say.

SETTING THE SCENE

London is the capital of England. It is the largest city in Europe, with an official population in 2012 of 8,308,400.[1] London is divided into 32 boroughs, plus the "City of London," the one-square-mile area enclosed by the ancient city boundary (see Figure 4.1). Up to 1990 the Inner London Education Authority (ILEA) administered 900 schools across the 12 Inner London boroughs, and each of the 20 Outer London boroughs had a separate local education authority (school district). After 1990, when the ILEA was abolished, each Inner London borough formed its own education authority, bringing the total to 32 local authorities, plus the City (governed by the Corporation of London), which is one of the world's financial capitals, with few residential properties and only one primary (elementary) school.

Buildup to Reforms

The big shake-up of London's schools started in 1990 when Prime Minister Margaret Thatcher's government abolished the ILEA as part of the Education Reform Act of 1988. After the ILEA was terminated, its 900

Figure 4.1. Map of London Distinguishing the 20 Outer London Boroughs from the 12 Inner London Boroughs and the City of London

schools were transferred to the 12 Inner London boroughs plus the City of London. While this was a big deal for those Inner London boroughs, it was eclipsed by other major reforms that transformed the whole English education system. We start by outlining some of the national context that is significant for the later London reforms of 2002–2012.

Tories: Choice and Diversity

In the same 1988 legislation, the government established the first national curriculum for England. Local education authority (school district) advisers provided essential support to schools. In the 12 Inner London boroughs, where the ILEA was fading out and the new administrations did not start until 1990, schools were left to fend for themselves. While implementing the national curriculum was a huge task for school principals, it was familiar work. But the 1988 Education Reform Act also introduced local management of schools, shifting money from local education authorities (LEAs) to school governing bodies. Even in well-run LEAs, this breathtaking legislation created confusion. It is hard to imagine what it must have felt like to be a primary school principal in a tough Inner London school where the normal daily challenges were immense and the LEA was in limbo.

Overall, the 1988 education reforms increased national government bureaucracy and diminished LEA powers. The Thatcher government purposefully set about centralizing control and replacing education as a public service with a school market for parental choice. The national curriculum included national tests for all students and school test scores were published in newspapers. Parents had free choice about which school to send their children to. School budgets were based on student numbers and the policy was designed so that good schools would flourish, while those with poor results would close. It seems likely that these reforms had a big influence on Bloomberg and Klein in NYC (see Chapter 2).

The 1988 Education Reform Act also created City Technology Colleges (CTCs)[2] for inner-city areas with enhanced budgets to serve deprived students. These new high schools were equipped with the most up-to-date resources and staffed with the best teachers in the system. Many would agree with this in equity terms, and it gave the policy some moral authority. However, CTC's explicit mission was to compete with and outperform neighboring high schools run by LEAs. In a market-based school system, it was easy to predict the eventual outcome, especially when CTCs had the edge in terms of funding, resources, and teachers. Surrounding high schools feared they would become "sink schools" (schools left to cope with the most challenging students in a spiral of decline). For various reasons the program ground to a halt and only 15 CTCs were built, but they were the forerunners of charter schools in the United States and academies in England. It is worth referring back to our push–pull dynamic framework at this point, since this attempted reform is a good example. Few people would challenge the moral imperative to put more resources into schools that serve our most disadvantaged students. But because the government tried to impose this on the system, without even consulting local communities where these schools were to be built, it failed. Too much push and not enough pull.

The Conservative government continued with successive waves of education reform through the 1990s. They had two common features: reducing spending on public education and promoting a radical policy of choice and diversity. When the CTC program failed, the government returned to the drawing board and came back with specialist technology colleges. Existing secondary schools were allowed to bid for specialist status, based loosely on magnet school ideas from the United States. If successful, schools received significant additional funds channeled through a new bureaucracy called the Specialist Schools Trust set up by the government. This further weakened LEA influence on its high schools.

By fragmenting the system and removing local authority control over schools, the government needed a more robust accountability system to monitor standards. The Office for Standards in Education (Ofsted) was established in 1993 to inspect all schools in England through a system of external audit by regulated independent inspectors. Inspection reports were published and pilloried failing schools. While Ofsted increased pressure on schools and provided additional accountability, it gave parents more reliable information than raw test data. Nevertheless, the inspection process is stressful and preparation is very time-consuming for teachers. With all this energy diverted from teaching, it was no surprise that school standards slipped.

Concern grew over the state of public education, particularly the rising inequality between rich and poor. In 1991 Sir Claus Moser, president of the British Association for the Advancement of Science, called for a Royal Commission to review education and training.[3] When the government refused, the philanthropic Paul Hamlyn Foundation stepped in to sponsor a private National Commission instead. The National Commission identified underachievement in economically deprived areas as an acute problem. The performance gap between schools in low-income areas and other areas was wide and increasing. To argue the case that poverty is an unacceptable excuse for low achievement, the National Commission reported about highly successful schools in poor communities throughout the United Kingdom.[4] But these were isolated schools surrounded by many more schools that were underperforming.

New Labour: Diversity and Excellence

In 1997 the Conservatives were defeated by New Labour with Tony Blair elected as prime minister. Opponents of the Conservative reforms breathed a sigh of relief. But not for long. Blair was influenced by the National Commission, and in his election campaign he announced that his three priorities in government would be education, education, and education. Despite concerns about widening performance gaps between rich and poor, the Blair government's first education priority was focused on the entire primary (elementary) school system. Class sizes were reduced for 5- to 7-year-olds. The National Literacy Strategy (NLS) in 1998 was followed by the National Numeracy Strategy (NNS) a year later. The sound bite was "Standards not Structures." Through these reforms, the government centralized control over teaching in 20,000 primary schools by prescribing daily lesson plans for literacy and numeracy. Teachers were trained by government-paid consultants, who in turn were regimented by tightly scripted training programs and inspected by Ofsted. It was extreme uniformity, which was one reason why the reforms ran out of steam. Strangely, the same government was preaching about the virtues of diversity in high schools.

Schools were expected to set ever-increasing annual targets in the national tests. Test results at the end of Year 6 (11-year-olds) improved rapidly from 1997 to 2000, then stalled and leveled off. Evaluation of NLS/NNS by the Ontario Institute for Studies in Education (OISE) suggested that in order to respond to future challenges, teachers needed deeper understanding through more professional learning.[5] The national strategies carried on until 2011, with marginal improvements in test scores after 2000.

The Blair government reinforced some of the education reforms initiated by the Conservatives, particularly in secondary schools. The slogan changed from "Choice and Diversity" to "Diversity and Excellence," and the government commitment to school performance tables, competition, and parental choice between schools remained the same. There were more financial incentives for secondary schools to specialize. The target-obsessed government set itself a target to approve 650 new specialist schools by 2001. These schools were allowed to select 10% of their intake by students' aptitude in a particular subject. Local authorities had no direct control over any of their schools unless they failed an Ofsted inspection. Despite this, in many areas, particularly in the urban districts, they developed strong and effective partnerships with their schools, characterized by collaboration, mutual trust, and respect.

In response to the challenges faced by schools in urban areas, where the Labour government had its core supporters, the government announced the creation of Education Action Zones (EAZs) in 1998. It was an idea copied from France and had three strands: partnerships between education and the private sector, collaboration across a network of schools, and innovation.[6] The EAZ policy suffered from light government monitoring and clumsy implementation. In terms of our dynamic framework, this was a different imbalance: a case of too much pull and not enough push. The program was abandoned before the zones had run their course, although the funding continued for 5 years.[7] When the 73 EAZs were eventually evaluated after 5 years, high school test results increased in one zone, decreased in two zones, and remained static in the rest.[8]

In 1999 the EAZ policy was replaced by the Excellence in Cities (EiC) program. With all primary schools fully engaged in the numeracy and literacy strategies, EiC was initially only for secondary schools in the most deprived districts. These were also the districts with the lowest test scores. Schools and the local authority formed partnerships to implement the program, which had three compulsory strands in all schools:

- Learning Mentors—to support students at risk of underachieving or losing interest in school and learning
- Learning Support Units—to provide short-term respite in school for students at risk of being excluded, usually through bad behavior

- Gifted and Talented—to develop enrichment activities to help high-performing students reach their full potential

Although the overall program was not negotiable, schools and LEAs had flexibility to determine how to plan and organize each strand—a reasonable push–pull balance. Evaluation by the London School of Economics and inspections by Ofsted show that the EiC program was successful at improving students' attendance but had only a marginal impact on their attainment.[9]

The New Labour government created the National College for School Leadership (NCSL) in 2000 with a plan to develop research and provide training and other learning opportunities for a wide range of leaders in schools, not just headteachers (principals). This was the first college in the world uniquely dedicated to the professional development of school leaders.

Suspicions that the Blair government was really the Tories in disguise as far as education was concerned were strengthened in 2000 when the CTC idea of private schools funded by the taxpayer returned like a boomerang. The New Labour government called them "City Academies." Initially city academies were styled as a radical approach to break the cycle of failing schools in inner cities. Later they were built in rural areas and "'city'" was dropped from the title. Businesses, churches, or voluntary groups can sponsor an academy. In return for a £2 million ($3.1 million) donation to the capital costs (in many cases never paid), sponsors own the buildings and control the school. All the running costs come directly from the government. Academies receive more funding than other schools in the district, as they take a share of the administration costs away from the local authority. In order to drive this policy forward, after 2002 all new secondary schools built by the government had to be academies.

Blair was elected for a second term in 2001, and the government seemed hell-bent on abolishing comprehensive high schools. In 2002 Estelle Morris, the Secretary of State for Education, announced that the days of the one-size-fits-all local comprehensive school were over when she set new targets to increase the number of specialist schools. It was a reversal of the 1997 policy based on "Standards not Structures." Its own watchdog, the Education Select Committee, criticized the government for spending £400 million ($613 million) on specialist schools without any evidence that they were working. After collecting evidence from expert witnesses, the Select Committee concluded that the emphasis on choice had resulted in a serious mismatch of expectations. The rhetoric on choice had not been matched by reality for parents.[10]

In London and other urban areas good public transport meant that parents had an illusion of choice between high schools within reasonable traveling distance. In reality, the schools chose the students according to a set of rules that favored the well-informed and middle-class parents. Sir Tim Brighouse, London's schools commissioner, describes it vividly:

> I saw the way these secondary admissions operated in London—with many quasi-selective schools setting their own entry criteria—producing a set of secondary schools that collectively resembled not so much a marketplace of individual competing shops that parents could choose to use, but more a hierarchy of private clubs ranging from the Carlton Club at one extreme and the East Cheam Working Men's Club on the other.[11]

Prime Minister Blair epitomized the process when his children transferred from primary to secondary schools while he was in office. Both his sons traveled across London daily to attend the exclusive London Oratory School.

London 1990–2002

After the breakup of the ILEA, schools in the 12 Inner London boroughs faced the normal challenges of urban education and also dealt with the government-mandated changes outlined above. Some schools and some boroughs coped better than others. When the results of the first national tests were published in 1996, five Inner London boroughs were among the lowest-performing LEAs across the country, with Tower Hamlets and Hackney at the bottom. These boroughs also had the highest rates of unemployment, poverty, crime, and social deprivation in the country. We trace developments in these two boroughs through the decade 2002–2012 as they worked independently to resolve these issues. But first we describe just how bad things were to begin with.

Tower Hamlets. Located east of the City on the north bank of the river Thames, Tower Hamlets includes the old docklands from the 18th and 19th centuries when London grew as a world trading port. When the docks were booming, Tower Hamlets had a population of over 600,000—about the same as Boston today, but more densely packed into 7.6 square miles. The area was bombed heavily during World War II when 100,000 homes were destroyed. They were replaced by low-quality apartment blocks to house dock workers and their families after the war. The area went into dramatic economic and social decline in the late 1960s when the docks closed. By 1981, the population dwindled to 140,000, mostly out of work or on low incomes. Derelict factories and empty houses were icons of urban decay when the London Docklands Development Corporation was established to regenerate the depressed area.

On the other side of the world, cyclones and floods in 1988 and 1989 drove thousands of refugees to flee Bangladesh. Those arriving in London were housed in empty, council-owned properties in Tower Hamlets. Just as schools were transferred from ILEA to the local council, they were overwhelmed by thousands of new immigrants bringing few belongings and no money from tiny rural villages.

Headteachers who have worked in Tower Hamlets since the ILEA days recall how bad it was in 1990, with over 400 children out of school and no places for them.[12] But worse than that were the prevailing low educational expectations for indigenous East End kids that were deeply rooted within the schools and the local community. High school records show that less than 1% of students went on to any form of higher education. Low aspirations by teachers, students, and their parents were shamefully met.

The first local authority inspection by Ofsted in 1998 was very critical.[13] The new director, Christine Gilbert, was served a notice to improve. When Ofsted came back 2 years later, they reported substantial improvements across the system, although Tower Hamlets still had some way to go in terms of school performances.[14] Nevertheless, the borough narrowly escaped government intervention, and this in itself was a significant reason for its subsequent incredible trajectory.

Hackney. While Tower Hamlets had started to turn the corner by 2000, its East End neighbor Hackney was still in deep trouble. At the time, the Hackney Council was politically unstable. After an Ofsted inspection in 1997 reported that the local authority was failing its duties, the government forced the council to appoint an external Hackney Improvement Team (HIT). This was immediately dubbed the "HIT squad" and conflict escalated. Hackney was not the only local authority that Ofsted judged to be failing. Three other Inner London boroughs were in bad shape together with half a dozen more inner-city local authorities around the country. At the time the government had no powers to intervene, but legislation enabling government intervention soon passed through Parliament without serious opposition.

The HIT squad had no impact. After a second bad inspection report the government intervened again in Hackney. In 1999 the council's school improvement service went out for bid and a 3-year contract was awarded to a private company. The crunch came in 2000 when the Audit Commission reviewed the council's overall finances and reported that it was bankrupt.[15] If things continued, they were heading for a £40 million ($65 million) debt. All spending, including that in schools, was frozen.

Hackney replaced Tower Hamlets as the lowest-performing local authority in the country. But unlike Tower Hamlets, there was no effective leadership for education in Hackney and the council was so divided it was incapable of making any sensible decision. After yet another inspection by Ofsted, the government intervened a third time, but privatization of the school improvement service in Hackney was not showing any impact on school performance. The preferred solution in Hackney was to set up the first nonprofit private company, The Learning Trust (TLT), to run education services for an entire borough. It was a political win-win, as it appealed to the Right, who claimed it would rescue the poor children in Hackney from the hopeless local council, and to the Left, who declared it was the end of the line for profit-making privatization of education. The Learning Trust was awarded a 10-year contract to run education in Hackney from 2002. What happened next was described as "a revolution in a decade."[16]

LONDON CHALLENGE

London Challenge, initiated by the national government in 2003, was a set of actions that focused on the development of the teaching and leadership capacity of London educators to improve the system. As such, London Challenge had no legal authority over the boroughs or schools, but did have resources and respected leadership that resulted in new levels of collaborative work.

In 2002 five London LEAs were consistently the lowest-performing local authorities in the country. The government had already intervened in all five boroughs, privatizing services to different degrees. Then in 2003 Blair announced London Challenge to improve standards in secondary schools across London, but particularly in these five boroughs, possibly the most unlikely systemwide endeavor ever attempted, as there had never been any coordination of education across the 33 London boroughs and local authorities had no direct control over their secondary schools anyway. If we think about our dynamic push–pull framework, we realize that it was difficult for London Challenge to be pushy, as it had no formal powers. Instead, its actions were predominantly on the pull side of the dynamic. So how could it achieve any balance? Read on.

Estelle Morris, the government Secretary of State for Education at the time, persuaded Sir Tim Brighouse to lead London Challenge as commissioner for London's schools. It was an inspired appointment. Brighouse had just retired as Chief Education Officer for Birmingham, England's second-largest city, with a successful track record. Earlier in his career he cut his teeth as an education officer with the ILEA, so that gave him street credibility in the capital. Perhaps most important was Brighouse's rapport with teachers. Morris appointed a junior minister, Stephen Twigg, as minister for London schools, and together with a handful of civil servants, they set about devising London Challenge and attempting a systemwide reform without any control of the system.

London Challenge, initially for secondary schools, had four simple themes:

- The London teacher
- The London leader
- The London school
- The London student

The London Teacher

Recruitment and retention of teachers is a bigger challenge in London than elsewhere in England. The turnover is higher, and there are more unqualified teachers.[17] High house prices and rents make living in London unaffordable for teachers and other key workers in the public sector such as nurses, social workers, and police. Although not a specific policy for London Challenge, the government introduced the Key Worker Living scheme in 2004 to help resolve the housing problems. Prior to that, some local authorities, like Hackney and Tower Hamlets, offered affordable rented accommodation for its workforce. This support was retained in these boroughs even after the government transferred employer responsibility from districts to individual schools.

London Challenge introduced the Chartered London Teacher (CLT) award in 2004.[18] This recognizes and rewards the skills and expertise of London's teachers. It takes 2 years from registration to gain the award, which is based on evidence from job-embedded professional learning. It carried a lump-sum payment of £1,000 ($1,550) and Fellowship of the College of Teachers for life. By 2007, some 40,000 teachers (two-thirds of London's teachers) were registered, and 200 had already gained the award with many more well on their way. The CLT was far more widespread than the five target boroughs, and it provided two benefits:

1. CLT aimed specific support and professional development at key issues in urban education.
2. CLT created a pool of qualified teachers to work with and help other colleagues in their own schools, helping to reduce variation within schools.

These actions are very clearly on the pull side of our dynamic framework—developing professional power. To achieve balance, London Challenge worked on the principle that if you are a big dog, then you don't need to bark. What we mean is that the balancing push came from Ofsted, which created the high sense of urgency through its inspections and published reports. London Challenge did not need to duplicate this. We see here how the reform attempted to compensate for an imbalance that pre-existed in the system. This counterbalance also applies to Keys to Success, which we describe below.

The London Leader

Teachers in England have a range of leadership responsibilities that carry additional pay. In secondary schools there are team leaders and heads of subject departments with responsibility for planning, organizing, coaching, monitoring, and evaluating work of fellow teachers. There is a clear leadership progression from teacher leader, subject leader, and senior leader to headteacher (principal). In London Challenge, the leadership theme covered the wide range of leadership roles. Successful headteachers were released part-time from their own schools to work with London Challenge on these four leadership strands:

1. Coaching teacher leaders and subject leaders in a program called "leading from the middle."
2. Designing and organizing 2-day retreats for leadership teams from challenged schools, giving them time away from the pressures of routine school business to resolve school issues and develop trust in one another.
3. Brokering two or three school visits for newly appointed middle or senior leaders between their appointment and taking up their post to stimulate new thinking and broaden their vision.
4. Training and deploying consultant heads. This was the most effective strand and we see how it was applied in the next section. It was so successful that it was adapted by NCSL, turned into the National Leader of Education program, and applied across the country.

The London School

There were two parts to this theme: the Keys to Success schools and Families of Schools.

Keys to Success Schools

Some secondary schools across London had long histories of staffing shortages, poor performance, and chronic low morale. They staggered from one crisis to another, firefighting all the way. These schools were expected to wither and perish in a competitive free-market school system. The odds were stacked against them by the actions of other schools, which rigged the system in their own favor by covert selection procedures. These were the last-resort schools with empty places for the most recently arrived refugees, asylum seekers from the world's latest war, plus children in poverty. And there was always room for more troublesome students excluded by other schools. These were the Keys to Success schools. Tim Brighouse explains why:

> We reasoned that it was counter-productive to blame the victim—in this case the school with the biggest task in breaking the link between poverty and (low) educational performance. If they could do it, we argued, any school should be able to do the same. The back of our self-imposed task would be broken. We therefore dubbed the schools "Keys to Success" and set about the complex task of helping them.[19]

We pause here to draw attention to a subtle choice of words in Brighouse's statement that has very important implications. He says, "If *they* could do it . . . any school should be able to do the same." The purposeful action is about helping the schools to improve themselves; it is not about someone outside the school turning it around. There is a subtle balance in the dynamics. Intervention is a very pushy action.

Recognizing that each school is unique, there were no prescribed solutions in the Keys to Success program. London Challenge recruited eight part-time school improvement advisers to bring in extra help for half a dozen Keys to Success schools each. The advisers worked in partnership with the school and the local authority, which in most cases was already working with the school. Their key strength was their skill at matching people to schools and creating a sense of mutual trust. It was important that schools felt London Challenge was working with them and not imposing solutions on them. London Challenge offered a range of additional support, according to the school's own diagnosis, such as the following:

- Additional leaders to work in school for a short term
- Regular help from advanced skills teachers
- Extra tutorial support and coaching for students about to take examinations
- New computers and IT equipment
- Support from consultant heads who were trained under the London Leader theme
- Help with removing leaders who could not cope

Over 5 years London Challenge supported more than 70 Keys to Success schools at three levels: light touch, maintained, or intensive support. Rather than supply additional money to the school budget, London Challenge paid for the support directly, ensuring that the money was used as intended. Typically, London Challenge spent between £30,000–£50,000 ($45,000–$80,000) on each Keys to Success school.[20] These were wise investments, and Ofsted recognized the long-term benefits in their inspection of London Challenge: "Schools that have improved and left the 'Keys to Success' program of London Challenge have developed robust systems to track pupils' progress and provide effective intervention for pupils at risk of underachievement."[21]

There is a slight twist to the way London Challenge fits into our dynamic framework in Keys to Success. The supports provided to struggling schools are clearly pulling actions to improve professional power, and they were never pushed on any school. The school had to work out its own solutions and ask for the help it needed. As already noted, the push was coming from Ofsted, as these were mostly failing schools. However, London Challenge was also pushy, but not with the struggling schools. Instead, London Challenge pushed the successful schools in the system to help and challenged the status quo that way. And of course it had the courage to intervene when many people would have preferred to close the struggling schools. London Challenge realized that this was a false solution, as the students in these schools would be transferred to other schools that might or might not be able to cope with them. The surest way to improve the system was to deal with the schools as they were.

Families of Schools

London Challenge produced a sophisticated statistical analysis of all examination results in all secondary schools across London.[22] It was published annually from London Challenge's 2nd year. Each school was put into a statistical family according to its student intake in terms of their prior attainment at age 11 and socioeconomic profile. Families of Schools cut across local authority boundaries. Schools could compare their progress in each subject with other schools from a similar start-up. Rather than compete with one another in a league table, schools were encouraged to work collaboratively within their families in order to narrow gaps and improve standards. Brighouse claims it is hard to overestimate the importance of the Families of Schools reports.[23] Later, a version was produced for primary schools. According to the Ofsted inspection:

> The leaders of London Challenge have motivated London teachers to think beyond their intrinsic sense of duty to serve pupils well within their own school and to extend that commitment to serving all London's pupils well.

This has encouraged successful collaboration between London school leaders and teachers across schools. This is a key driver for improvement.[24]

London Challenge developed a widespread sense among London teachers that they were all in it together, working with one another across and between schools. This was noted in the Ofsted evaluation: "Their sense of pride in being part of a citywide education service, irrespective of whether they were receiving or providing support, was a fundamental characteristic of London Challenge."[25] It is worth remembering that these were schools working across local authority boundaries. It shows that organizational structures are less important than actions when it comes to leadership across a system. It was through these pulling actions that London Challenge exerted its leadership rather than by any formal structure.

The London Student

Like other big cities, London has many historic buildings, art galleries, museums, concert halls, theaters, and sports facilities. They attract tourists from around the globe. Most parents living in the city enjoy the cultural enrichment opportunities available to them and their children. Yet many children from low-income families never benefit. London Challenge tackled this inequality through the "student pledge." The student pledge listed a minimum set of experiences that each secondary student should enjoy in or out of school. Schools were encouraged to sign up to the pledge and build these opportunities into the curriculum. It was a symbolic way of showing that what is good enough for privileged children should be experienced by everyone. London Challenge worked with providers to gain free or subsidized access for London students.

London Student Achievement, 2004-2012

All students in England are expected to take General Certificate of Secondary Education (GCSE) examinations at the end of Year 11 when they are 16 years old. That is the completion of compulsory education, although youngsters continue learning at school, in work, or at community college until they are 18. There are separate, externally marked, exams for each subject they study during Years 10 and 11; students may take GCSE exams in 10 or 11 different subjects. Students are graded from A* to G according to their marks in each exam. The benchmark is to make a grade of C or higher in at least five different subjects, which must include English and mathematics. School performance tables rank schools, local authorities, and regions according to the percentage of 16-year-olds who achieve this benchmark. It is the equivalent of graduation in English secondary schools.

Figure 4.2 shows the improvement across the Inner London boroughs from 34% to 61% that lifted the average for the most deprived parts part of the city from well below to just over the national average. It is much better than the general trend for England, and this feeds into the overall London rates. While these data do not indicate cause and effect, they do show important systemwide improvements across London, particularly the most deprived parts of London. Comparing the socioeconomic profiles of students in London with England overall, it provides compelling evidence that poverty is no excuse for low performance.

EAST END BOROUGHS OF TOWER HAMLETS AND HACKNEY

So far we have covered the government's attempts to drive improvement through the overall system and discussed how London Challenge took that further within the most deprived parts of the system. Yet none of this gives us a real sense of how system leaders came to grips with the overwhelming challenges in order to make the improvements evident in Figure 4.2. We now study the improvements in the two East End boroughs of Hackney and Tower Hamlets in more depth for three reasons:

Figure 4.2. Percentage of 16-Year-Old Students Achieving at Least Five GCSE Grades A*–C, Including English and Mathematics, for England, London, and Inner London, from 2004 to 2012

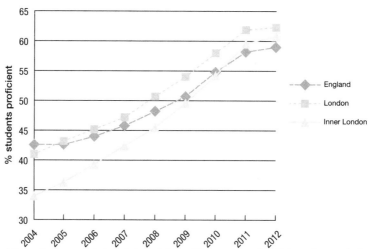

Note: All performance data retrieved from Department for Education website: www.education.gov.uk/schools/performance/

1. These are the most deprived parts of London and England and at different times each borough was the lowest-performing school district in the country.
2. By 2012, schools in both boroughs performed above the national averages.
3. By taking two case studies in detail, we can examine actual strategies and dynamics of change up close.

Using Brighouse's reasoning for Keys to Success, if these districts can make systemwide improvements, then any district should be able to do the same. But we remember that just like the Keys to Success schools, each school district is unique, and there are no prescribed solutions. Even so, we can learn from how they did it as well as from what they did. Just as the people inside a failing school are responsible for its recovery, the same goes for turnaround systems. While London Challenge offered additional resources, it was the system leaders and school leaders in Tower Hamlets and Hackney who turned these districts around.

Tower Hamlets (42,000 students in 97 schools)

In 1998 Ofsted gave Christine Gilbert the equivalent of a final written warning—improve or else. Her first two years as Director of Education were probably no more important than the rest, but at the time they were crucial. When she arrived in Tower Hamlets, there were effective systems in place, but relationships between the local authority and its schools were strained by the hard-line approach of the advisory service. Gilbert's previous experience was important in two ways. She already had a successful track record as Director of Education in one of the Outer London boroughs and before that she had been a successful headteacher. Tower Hamlets headteachers immediately recognized her as one of them and Gilbert won them over by listening, taking account of what they were saying, and then acting on it. She created a better balance between challenging the status quo and working out a commonly owned strategy. Previously there was too much push and not enough pull.

The study of Tower Hamlets was originally a small part of the Performance Beyond Expectations research led jointly by Andy Hargreaves from Boston College and Alma Harris from London Institute of Education.[26] To explain how systemwide improvements were secured, we describe four characteristics that are widely shared by educators in Tower Hamlets, whether they work in schools or at the district level:

- Resolute leadership
- Allegiance

- Professional power
- Sustainability

In our dynamic framework language, resolute leadership operates as a push factor, allegiance serves to pull people together, professional power has aspects of both push and pull, and sustainability is essentially the pull of new implementation. Together the four factors provide an integrated balance of conditions favorable to continuous change.

Resolute Leadership

Tower Hamlets has developed an achievement culture focused on action. They set pushy targets, stick to their core principles, and skillfully combine short-term gains in test scores with long-term goals for student achievement. Excuses and blame are sidestepped if targets are missed; the system learns and moves on.

Christine Gilbert's greatest gift to Tower Hamlets was to raise expectations. She avoided the comfort of contextual value-added measures that showed how well they were doing compared with other high-poverty districts, when in reality too many students were failing their tests. Coming from a high-performing Outer London borough, Gilbert insisted that students in Tower Hamlets were just as capable as students elsewhere. They might need some extra help to get there, but they could still make the grade on time. Today that belief is widespread, and Tower Hamlets students beat the national averages. And those high expectations extend to staff as well as students. According to one of the service heads in the district, "We all believed we could make a difference. And in any case Christine expected us to—so we did." In this respect, challenging the status quo, Gilbert was a very pushy leader.

Schools were encouraged to make realistic predictions of students' test scores based on their prior attainment and current progress. That was the baseline. Then they were asked to set more ambitious targets based on what students might achieve if they were given some specific additional help. These were not dreams they might aspire to like winning the lottery, but achievable targets they could reach with extra support or more hard work. Schools then had two levels to reach—predicted and target. When the results came in, headteachers had a conversation with their district adviser. Most schools' test scores fell somewhere between the predicted and target levels. There was no blame attached to failing to meet their ambitious targets, just a learning conversation. Of course, that conversation was more important if a school missed its predicted level. Here we find a great balance between using data to create more urgency around students' needs and pulling in the professional power to meet them.

Working this way, Tower Hamlets collected detailed information about all the additional support schools needed to meet their ambitious targets. That was used to plan the district's school-improvement support based on teachers' diagnoses of students' needs. Consequently, the local authority's action plan gave a real sense of purpose and became its highest priority. In an ideal world the plan gets implemented and things progress smoothly. Life is never that simple in the real world. Things happen that will tend to pull organizations in other directions, like new government initiatives. It takes resolute leadership to refuse because it would deflect energy and effort away from the priority action plan— built on students' real needs and geared to ambitious targets. It is tough to stick to your core activities in the ebb and flow of changing circumstances. But having done so and won through, it boosts your confidence. So it is that schools in Tower Hamlets will not be deflected from their essential work by superfluous government policies. If it fits in with their core priorities, they will consider it; otherwise they refuse. A refusal, for example, occurred in relation to city academies that we discuss below under allegiance.

Allegiance

Allegiance among educators in Tower Hamlets is a compelling characteristic that fosters a sense of belonging. It grew from desperation in daunting times and developed into a tradition. It is nurtured by trust and respect. It surpasses self-interest because it realizes that mutual benefits are wider and more long-lasting. In Tower Hamlets there is an authentic collective responsibility that breeds loyalty and commitment. These are very strong pulling actions around a commonly owned strategy. But where is the balancing push to provide the challenge? That is a surprising element we find later under Professional Power.

Many Prime Ministers and royalty have visited the outstanding Morpeth School in Tower Hamlets. It's a great photo opportunity for visitors. Headteacher Sir Alasdair Macdonald was very clear about how allegiance had a huge part to play in the systemwide improvements in Tower Hamlets.[27] For example, he explained why secondary heads in Tower Hamlets resisted the government's attempts to build a city academy in the borough. In his long and distinguished career in education, he could not recall how the selective improvement of one school, or one type of school, does anything to improve the system. In fact, as he saw in other districts, it contributed to the breakup of the system. As there had been no desire in Tower Hamlets to break away from the local authority, why would that change in favor of a city academy? Their collective view was that a city academy posed more of an overall threat to the life chances of students in

Tower Hamlets than a benefit, although it might benefit a few students in one school at the expense of the rest. An unusual balance is here in terms of our dynamic framework. The schools show courage to be quite pushy against the government policy in order to pull together more in the interests of sustainability. In other words, leaders in Tower Hamlets were low on complacence for the sake of compliance and high on influencing one another for the sake of children's learning.

Professional Power

Systemwide improvements rely on professional power, which is generated by using available resources with determination and persistence. Tower Hamlets directed all its resources to achieve high impact. They included merging budgets to increase outcomes. Council resources augmented those in the community. Professional skills were enhanced by confidence, determination, and competition to compound success. With persistence, professional power generated momentum that carried the system through unexpected challenges. It is the system-level equivalent of capacity building in schools.

Tower Hamlets is no different from any other efficient local authority when it comes to handling its budget. What sets it apart is the way it created synergy with other resources in the community. Local authority leaders reached out to the corporate sector to find partners who were eager to respond. Tower Hamlets linked each school with a big-city firm through a formal agreement. It wasn't financing that the local authority was seeking; it was something more valuable than that. The business leaders were committed to make a difference but needed leadership from the LEA about how best to assist schools. Bringing business expertise into each school obviously expanded the leadership capacity at school level. But it was more direct links with students that had immediate impact. Four thousand volunteers went into schools each week to help youngsters read, play chess, or do mathematics. LEA consultants trained the volunteers in the things they should be doing in school. Christine Gilbert was convinced that the real value was not so much in the help with reading or mathematics but more in the personal connection between each child and an adult. Someone who was going to focus individual attention on that child for a whole hour improved the self-esteem and intrinsic motivation of the student. Interestingly, it had similar benefits for the mentors.

District and school leaders engaged productively with community leaders, especially those in the mosques. They worked in partnership to dismantle cultural barriers that hampered students' learning. For example, the council funded an attendance project through the London Muslim Center. Outreach workers from the community encouraged parents to send their children to school as part of their duty as good Muslims. The practice of sending children for extended holidays to visit their ancestral homeland during term time was discouraged by community leaders.

The competitive edge in the borough was more elusive, especially when collaboration between schools was such an important feature. But it was there under the surface. With so many high-poverty and high-performing schools and a culture of no excuses, the unspoken message was if the school next door can beat the national average then we are determined to do the same, or better. This was the balancing push that provides the challenge we referred to earlier. It is surprising because it emerges between the schools themselves pushing one another; it does not rely on being challenged by system leaders. When that determined and competitive attitude was blended with genuine collaboration, then the system exhibited professional power. This kind of competition is more about beating your personal best than winning at all costs or belittling others. When schools shared good ideas and best practices, they were contributing to the greater good, which increased their self-actualization and pride in the system.

The last part of this characteristic is persistence. Professional power must be sustained across the system and over time to achieve the kind of system-level improvements displayed by Tower Hamlets. As successful strategies were spread around the system and extraordinary efforts became the norm, improved performance gathered momentum. Persistence meant there was no going back. Professional power energized the system, which created new ideas and opportunities to improve. With schools working together this way, supported by the LEA, systemwide improvements were secured. The fourth characteristic ensured they were continuous.

Sustainability

Four aspects of work in schools and at LEA level ensured the continued improvement in performance for Tower Hamlets. The four parts to sustainability were: recruitment, professional learning, attention to detail, and innovation.

Recruiting good people does more to sustain success than anything else. The situation today is very different from what it was when Tower Hamlets took over the schools from the ILEA. Back then there were not enough schools or teachers for the huge growth in student numbers. And outsiders were not attracted to work in challenging schools at the wrong end of the performance tables. Recruitment has always been a high priority for the borough and remains so. Finding good headteachers was even more important than recruiting new teachers. It was essential for Tower Hamlets to keep their best people and grow their own school leaders.

The investment paid off quickly, as they made fewer weak appointments. The borough used the same strategy to create a more diverse workforce to resemble the school community. Local people were trained to become teaching assistants. If successful, there were more opportunities through school-based training to become qualified teachers. The pathways for Bengalis through this route were very successful. Tower Hamlets now has one of the most vibrant and diverse teaching forces in the country. Good recruitment and growing their own talent gave Tower Hamlets a secure foundation for sustainability.

Good professional learning was the next ingredient. Having a young teaching force helped because inexperienced teachers were more likely to try new ideas and ways of working. They were less likely to be cynical and resist change. The borough devised its own leadership courses for the national headteachers' qualification in partnership with NCSL. All new headteachers were allocated a leadership coach from the private sector, paid for by the LEA for a year. There was no agenda, and it was up to the headteacher to make the most from their business mentor. The most effective professional learning grew out of collaboration, and Tower Hamlets would be recognized as a true professional learning community. For those schools that did get into trouble, there were well-developed systems of intensive support.

Sustaining improvement became more challenging as schools improved and performance soared. It was easier to improve from being the lowest-performing LEA than it was when close to the national average. At that stage Tower Hamlets needed to be much more diligent in seeking ways to improve when the majority of schools in the system were high-performing. This required even more attention to detail. Here we find another example of being pushy with data to find opportunities to pull in professional power and support students better.

Innovation was the last part of sustainability in Tower Hamlets, and that required risk taking. Any system has to take risks in order to innovate, but these were not the kind of risks that would jeopardize children's safety or their well-being. Instead it meant taking professional risks, trying out new ways of doing things, and encouraging schools to do the same. Innovation and risk taking flourished in the no-blame culture. Schools felt secure and strived to do better knowing that they would be supported if things did not work out.

Tower Hamlets gives us more insights into the subtlety and complexity of our simple dynamic framework of push and pull actions. When these were well balanced, they led to systemwide improvements. Balance, moreover, is not a once-only phenomenon; it must be carefully attended to over long periods of time. The final piece of the London case is about the East End neighboring borough of Hackney.

Hackney (36,000 students in 73 schools)

Alan Wood was appointed Director of Education by the Hackney Council in 2001. His job was to transfer the education system from the council to the private nonprofit company called The Learning Trust. He was previously director of another challenging Inner London borough and he arrived with a successful track record. Wood became the chief executive of The Learning Trust and provided the stable leadership that was desperately needed at the time. He continued to lead TLT throughout its existence.

As explained earlier, TLT started work in September 2002 with a 10-year contract, paid for by the government with money removed from Hackney Council. We draw heavily on an evaluation of TLT by Leannta Education Associates in 2012.[28] The focus of the study was to discover how TLT transformed education in Hackney to achieve systemwide improvements in performance. The complexity of the work over a decade makes it difficult to rate specific parts of the program in terms of their impact on school performances. Instead, the study reveals 10 characteristics of the way that TLT worked. The combination of these characteristics drove the systemwide improvements. The 10 characteristics are grouped into three themes:

- Commitment
- Capacity
- Confidence

There is nothing remarkable about these themes, but what we learn from them is how TLT improved performance and moved Hackney from being one of the most persistent low-performing boroughs to beating the national averages in a decade.

Commitment

At the beginning of a change process in a terribly performing system, the pursuit of commitment is more push than pull; that is, you have to start with the reality that commitment is low and insist that a key, nonnegotiable goal is to create the expectations and pursuit of widespread commitment to the new goals of the reform. In The Learning Trust commitment revealed two features: the conceptual identity of TLT and its consistency. It is remarkable that a fledgling organization could establish such a powerful identity in less than 10 years; it is a tribute to the leadership evident at all levels in TLT. Stable and consistent leadership combined with the TLT conceptual identity is what made the most difference.

Conceptual Identity. The Learning Trust is unique in England; there are no other private nonprofit companies administering schools for an entire borough. But just being different did not make TLT successful. TLT established a powerful identity that encompassed its values, beliefs, and way of working. After 10 years The Learning Trust brand was a collective identity that was widely shared. This was the driving force behind the commitment to transform Hackney's education system. It went way beyond mission statements, compelling visions, and inspirational dreams because it was based on action and reality. We illustrate the conceptual identity by exploring how it developed and the way TLT worked.

A contract with a private nonprofit company was the government's preferred solution to the crisis in Hackney. Instead of shareholders, the TLT Board was responsible to Hackney Council, which was acting on behalf of the residents in the borough. Rather than making financial profit, TLT was motivated to make intellectual profit in terms of the educational outcomes of young people in Hackney. Places on the board of nonexecutive directors were reserved for the Mayor, the Chief Executive of Hackney Council, and the Council's Lead Member for Children's Services. Other places were allocated to parents, headteachers, governors (members of individual school boards), and other stakeholders in the community. The government appointed the first chairman of the TLT Board. The three executive directors on the board were: Chief Executive, Director of Learning and Standards, and Director of Finance and Resources.

The length of the contract was an important consideration. Evidence from Ofsted showed that failing schools may be turned around in under 2 years, but that depended to some extent on how bad they were to begin with.[29] It takes longer to create sustainable improvements that produce outstanding schools. Systemwide change takes longer still.[30] The government also expected that any change process would be bumpy. Taking all this into consideration, a 10-year contract was probably the minimum length of time to give TLT a reasonable chance to show success.

Appointing Sir Mike Tomlinson as the first chair of The Learning Trust was a stroke of genius. He was approaching retirement from his post as head of Ofsted, after a highly successful and distinguished career in education. This was an important factor that got things off to a flying start. Estelle Morris, the government's Secretary of State for Education, acknowledges Tomlinson's credibility and the reasons for establishing TLT.

> By putting Mike in charge we were going back to our tried and tested educationalists, people like him who have credibility. We were trying to get school improvement in, not destroy the local authority. We wanted a nonprofit motive and to keep some semblance of local democracy. But more than that, the

golden rule was it had to be allowed to get on with improving education and could not be held back by failures elsewhere. We were trying to isolate it from the local authority but leave it enmeshed in the local community. The Learning Trust was the vehicle we chose to do that.[31]

One of Tomlinson's first tasks was to appoint the board of directors. The board quickly established an inspirational dream that everyone in Hackney wanted more than anything else: that in 10 years' time parents would struggle to get places for their children in Hackney schools. In 2002, when only 40% of parents sent their children to Hackney secondary schools, this was almost unimaginable; it was achieved by 2010.

The vision was not just exaltation; it led to action. The single-mindedness characterizes TLT. Unlike Hackney Council, which had responsibility for the administration of other public services, TLT had one purpose—education. This was an important feature of its success. Improving secondary schools was the first priority. It was important to engage with secondary headteachers in order to develop and implement the secondary school strategy, which had three clear priorities:

1. Recruit quality consultants; recruit quality leadership. Improve the existing schools.
2. Improve the existing school buildings. TLT used the government Building Schools for the Future (BSF) program to invest £170–£200 million ($260–$305 million) in seven secondary schools.
3. Build five new schools: the only way to achieve this was through the academies program.

The priorities are listed in order of their impact on school performance. Because it was clear that some high schools would be closed, it was vital for TLT to establish its integrity with the group of secondary headteachers. Straight away we see the importance of creating a commonly owned strategy, as shown in our dynamic framework. TLT leaders knew there would be tough times ahead when they needed to be very pushy, and it was important to pull everyone together first.

The combination of upgrading existing schools and building five brand-new academies was crucial physical evidence of the transformation in secondary education. Embracing the academy program was expedient rather than philosophical; it was the only way to build new schools. It relied on a strong partnership with Hackney Council. TLT engaged full support from Hackney Council with a set of guiding principles. Those principles laid down three conditions for building new academies in Hackney. TLT was very pushy about these principles, but mainly because it was the only way to keep the academies working together with the other schools.

1. Academy sponsors must show existing links with Hackney.
2. Hackney academies must commit themselves to the family of Hackney schools and agree not to select students.
3. Hackney academies could not be sponsored by churches or other faith groups.

A crucial part of the TLT secondary strategy was to close a failing school, disperse the students elsewhere, demolish the buildings, build a brand-new school on the land, open it with a new 1st-year intake, and allow the school to grow naturally year by year. They were completely new buildings, new staff, and new students. Each academy was able to establish a new culture from the start. TLT moved swiftly to close two failing schools and needed cooperation from the other secondary schools to disperse the students from the closing schools. When they were full, TLT created a temporary high school in a local college with first-class facilities, so these students immediately had a better deal.

The academy program threatened the other secondary schools that were improving. TLT worked hard to avoid creating a two-tier system. Nevertheless, the other secondary schools clearly needed to show they were not inferior in any way. By growing the academies one year at a time, it was not until 2009 that the first academy produced its first GCSE results. By then, the other Hackney secondary schools had improved so much that Hackney was already above the national average. This is an important point because some observers claim it was the academy program that improved secondary performance in Hackney. While the academies contributed to improvements after 2009, it was the other secondary schools in Hackney that provided liftoff.

The primary school sector was far more complex. There have always been some outstanding primary schools in Hackney, and that was true in 2002 when TLT was established. But they were outnumbered by primary schools with serious weaknesses and failing schools. The improvement strategy in primary schools was an intriguing blend of short-term and long-term strategies devised by Tricia Okoruwa when she was Deputy Director of TLT.

Okoruwa called the short-term strategy "Find & Fix"—for our dynamic framework, this is the courage to intervene (with data), and the corresponding building of commitment and capacity to fix the problem. Find & Fix was based on detailed analysis of school performance data to find groups of students that were at risk of not making the grade, particularly those in Years 5 and 6 (national tests are taken by all students at the end of Year 6). Here again we find the balance between being pushy with the data and pulling schools by providing additional support. TLT worked with headteachers to provide a wide range of additional help to accelerate these students' learning—booster classes, breakfast clubs, after-school coaching, and summer schools. She called the long-term strategy "Predict & Prevent." This was based on more general research about issues such as the impact of poverty on student achievement. TLT invested heavily in preschool provision and in the early years of primary education. There was a huge community initiative, led by TLT, to get all children reading before they were 7 years old. Find & Fix is about being pushy and intervening, balanced by Predict & Prevent, which is more of a pulling action that attends to sustainability. It is a great balanced strategy.

These were not particularly innovative strategies, but they had a clear rationale that was well balanced. The most impressive thing is the way they were implemented together, knowing that results from Predict & Prevent would take years to show through and, at the same time, dealing with the unexpected, which came in the form of schools failing Ofsted inspections. Responding to crises like these is common practice in urban school districts and is usually referred to as "firefighting." The danger is that the district support services are overwhelmed by firefighting and never get to Find & Fix, or find time to even think about Predict & Prevent. For sure, during its first five years TLT was heavily involved in firefighting and Find & Fix, but the long-term investment in Predict & Prevent eventually paid off.

The Learning Trust made significant improvements in both primary and secondary schools to begin with. That was essential because the initial standards were so low and, although not easy, there were a lot of gains to be made. Pushing performance further ahead required a step-change in terms of strategy and support. That occurred midway through the decade when the primary and secondary strategies were joined and the drive was to ensure that every school was a "Good" school. (In Ofsted terms, schools are judged on a 4-point scale: Poor, Satisfactory, Good, and Outstanding.) Being "Satisfactory" was not enough. To achieve that, TLT put much more emphasis on improving instruction, as we see later.

Consistency. The second feature of commitment was consistency. Time is a limiting factor for consistency. In order to prove its consistent support to schools, TLT needed time. The improvements over the decade show that TLT had sufficient time to develop a consistent and reliable service. While time is crucial, on its own it does not guarantee consistent improvements. What were the important features that enabled The Learning Trust to develop consistently high standards across Hackney?

Stable leadership would be no surprise. Alan Wood guided the system throughout. After serving as chief executive of TLT, he returned to Hackney Council in 2011 as Director of Children's Services to manage the transfer of education services back to the council at the end of TLT's contract.

Woods's sustained leadership is a critical factor in this transformation. Once appointed, all the senior leaders in TLT continued to work for the company after their recruitment in the first couple of years when TLT was building its leadership team.

It was not only stable leadership at the top; it ran through the organization. Once the right people were recruited, they were developed and grew more committed to their work. Professional growth and capacity building were also consistent. After leadership and growth, the next consistent issue was the single focus on education. Without the involvement of elected politicians, whose priorities may not always be entirely about education, TLT made unpopular decisions and acted on them swiftly. The typical local authority political process, often characterized by lengthy periods of consultations and compromise, would hamper such concerted and direct action. The single focus on education also meant that TLT's budget could not be diverted to other aspects of the Council's work, as frequently happens in local authorities.

Stable leadership, professional growth, a single focus with a protected resource—all contributed to a consistent approach and support for school improvement. This is essentially how TLT helped schools in Hackney to achieve high performance.

Capacity

We use the word *capacity* to describe the collective abilities, skills, intellectual understanding, and resources within The Learning Trust and Hackney schools that are used to help students learn. While resources such as time, the number of people, and the financing available may be fixed or limited, TLT believed that the abilities, professional skills, and intellectual understanding of staff were unlimited and offered potential for growth. We learn how TLT increased capacity across schools in Hackney and also within its own organization through direct action enhanced by four separate characteristics: courage, challenge, creativity, and collaboration.

Courage. In 2002 capacity was very low because many key posts were vacant and also because the collective abilities across the entire workforce that was transferred from Hackney Council to TLT were weak. The Learning Trust soon recognized that some staff had outlived their usefulness and that the organization had no room for them. This was all part of TLT's refusal to accept second-best, and it is a clear illustration of why courage is essential in order to build capacity. TLT went on a talent-spotting mission around the schools and within the organization. Good people were nurtured, coached, and developed rapidly. There was an aspiring leaders program that found potential team leaders as well as deputies and headteachers. TLT cut its administrative staff and invested in professional learning programs to provide support at all levels in primary and secondary schools. A great balance of push and pull dynamics—having the courage to fire staff whose performance was weak and using the saved budget to develop the professional power and potential of those in the system.

Challenge. Support and coaching will improve professional skills and understanding, but sometimes the process is too slow. TLT used challenge to speed it up. On its own, challenge would alienate schools, but combined with support, as outlined above, it created a robust and balanced strategy that sits well with our push–pull dynamics. There was a loud and bold refusal to accept poverty as an excuse for low performance; the chair of the board described it as "ferocious assertion." The kind of attitude that forms comments like, "What can you expect from kids like this?" was immediately challenged. Alan Wood put it quite bluntly: "We dealt very hard with the nonsense."[32]

The Learning Trust acted swiftly at the first sign of school weakness. Without the kind of bureaucracy that slows down many local authority services, TLT was very nimble and made speedy interventions. Headteachers appreciated this because the approach was to support, not to blame or criticize. The same rigor was applied internally. When school performance dipped, there was a challenging internal inquiry to put things back on track. TLT encouraged schools to have high expectations of their students just as TLT had of the schools. And within schools, headteachers had high expectations of their teachers.

All this required considerable courage from people working for TLT. They were powerfully motivated to improve schools by challenging low performance. TLT made unpopular decisions when necessary and followed them through quickly. If the support did not work, then TLT acted in the interests of students first and removed senior staff responsible for failures. In itself, removing a headteacher does not improve a school. There is no guarantee that the next one will be any better. But rather than endure continuing low performance, TLT was courageous and stepped in. It was better to take the risk than put up with inadequate school leaders. The same approach was used with its own staff. In the first few years the turnover was high as staff in TLT were challenged and dismissed if they failed to respond. It was hard pruning to stimulate new growth. The most courageous decisions were around closing failing secondary schools. These schools had long histories of low performance, but the council had never managed to deal with them. TLT closed them one at a time. This sent a clear message to parents in the community that TLT would not tolerate school failure.

Creativity. The Learning Trust approach to building capacity was more than a combination of support and tough action, although both were essential. High performance was unlikely if schools continued doing the same as before. TLT called for fresh ideas, innovation, and change. TLT encouraged creativity by empowering staff to take risks and experiment. TLT expected its staff to take bold decisions and act on them. They would be responsible for the outcomes, but TLT would rather have them make a mistake than do nothing. The approach was to push people to their limits. If you didn't fail at something, then it probably meant you were not trying hard enough. One powerful example was with the government's national strategies in literacy and numeracy (NLS and NNS). After years of following the primary strategies without much impact, in 2009 the Deputy Director decided to ignore the government guidance and have Hackney create its own strategy. It proved to be the turning point in Hackney primary schools' performance, as we reveal below when we examine the data.

Collaboration. The final contributory factor to increasing capacity was through collaboration, and this occurred in three different ways:

1. Between The Learning Trust and Hackney Council
2. Between secondary schools
3. Across primary school federations.

At the start of TLT's contract, its relationship with Hackney Council was tense. Councilors were bruised by the public humiliation that the borough suffered. They resented the fact that TLT was running Hackney's schools for 10 years. TLT realized early on that they needed to collaborate closely with Hackney Council in order to improve schools, particularly secondary schools. Hackney Council owned all the school sites and TLT needed partnerships with the council and the academy sponsors in order to build five new academies. It is astonishing that TLT managed to pull this off in 10 years. Another local borough struggled for longer than that to build a single academy.

The secondary school strategy was the key to convincing parents in Hackney that things were different. With five new schools being built in a tight urban district and renovations in the other schools, the physical changes were obvious. TLT knew that it would never work without the cooperation of all secondary schools. Opposition to academies was strong in neighboring Tower Hamlets. But Hackney was different in many ways. The Chair of the Board and the Chief Executive established a secondary strategy team with all the headteachers. Meetings were held informally over dinner and business was discussed around the dinner table in a relaxed environment. The group soon bonded and the secondary strategy was developed by the team. It was the strength of this collaboration that carried it through. There was a genuine commitment in the group to making things better for Hackney students, not just those in "my" school.

The most compelling evidence about how collaboration increased capacity came from the primary school federations in Hackney. The first federation came after Holy Trinity Primary failed its Ofsted inspection and the headteacher resigned. TLT Deputy Director Tricia Okoruwa asked Sîan Davies, head of the outstanding St. John & St. James Primary, to hold the fort at Holy Trinity. Both schools are state elementary schools in Hackney. Between them, Okoruwa and Davies worked out a recovery plan for Holy Trinity. The plan was that Davies become "executive head" of both Holy Trinity and her own school, St. John & St. James. That enabled Davies to bring good teachers from her own school into Holy Trinity so they could model lessons and coach teachers. Or she could switch teachers from Holy Trinity to her school to see good teachers in action. It was intensive, job-embedded professional learning. Davies was able to repair Holy Trinity quickly by adapting the same successful systems that worked in her own school.

Even Davies could not provide this level of support for Holy Trinity and run two schools simultaneously. So Okoruwa and Davies developed a new job they called "head of school" and appointed two of Davies's outstanding teacher leaders to this position, one in each school. Each head of school has full responsibility for the daily running of classes, meeting parents, and school routines. Davies, as executive head, was their line manager with responsibilities such as strategic planning, leadership development, and professional learning across both schools.

TLT worked in partnership with Davies and provided all the additional support and backup she needed. It was a potent school improvement strategy. Holy Trinity made the fastest-ever turnaround, from being a failing school to a "Good" school in under 12 months. The question then was, what do we do now? Holy Trinity was in good shape, so Davies could have returned to St. John & St. James and carried on as before. But everyone preferred the way they were working together as two separate schools but with the same systems so they could interchange teachers. The outcome was to establish the schools jointly as a federation, with one governing body and Davies as executive head supported by the heads of school as described. Roles and responsibilities were formally agreed on, and Hackney's first federation was formed.

TLT worked with Davies's federation to turn around seven failing schools. Some of them preferred to remain in the federation because working with a larger faculty provided more professional learning opportunities. The federation grew to include five schools, all of them outstanding in their own right and completely different in character although they shared common systems. New leadership roles were created for teacher leaders who worked across the federation. Some heads of school have moved on to be headteachers in regular schools and some have set up new federations as executive heads. By 2012, four federations operated like this in Hackney. They have created a huge increase in capacity very quickly and with little additional cost. This is another example of our push–pull dynamic framework, working across all three sets of actions. The pushiness of challenging the status quo, using data to create urgency, and having courage to intervene is balanced by the pulling power of crafting a commonly owned strategy, developing professional power in the failing schools that is sustainable.

Confidence

Confidence was a crucial feature in the transformation. Back in 2002, confidence in Hackney schools had been battered. Over 60% of parents chose to send their children to secondary schools outside Hackney, and there were more who wanted to but could not find places in other schools. Morale and self-esteem in schools were very low. Budgets had been frozen because the council was bankrupt, buildings were crumbling, and schools were pilloried in the press for low performance. By 2012, confidence could not be better. Parents from other boroughs were struggling to get their children into Hackney secondary schools, and they were all oversubscribed. School performance was above the national average, there were five brand-new academies, and other schools were renovated. Teachers were proud to work in Hackney. What we learn is that increased confidence was not only an outcome of the improvement, it was a causal factor. TLT deliberately worked to improve confidence and that raised performance. The confidence-building strategy had two parts, communication and celebration.

Communication. The appointment of Sir Mike Tomlinson was a key factor. He was an education statesman and immediately established the credibility of The Learning Trust. Tomlinson set the tone from the start and quickly breathed inspiration into Hackney and restored hope. For Tomlinson the big issue was not to be heavy-handed. It was about building relationships. He convinced teachers and headteachers that they could do it, that TLT believed in them and would help them. It had a remarkable effect. Nobody had ever talked to people in Hackney that way before. They began to feel valued. Increasing confidence was about helping people show how good they were, not making them feel good. We already covered how challenging TLT was, and the balance between challenge and confidence was tricky. However, the combination of inspiration, relationships, challenge, and support restored faith and started to build confidence in Hackney. In other words, the balance of push and pull dynamics. We next learn how important good communication was to increasing confidence.

Realizing the importance of relationships with schools, TLT built a communications and marketing team by employing experts from the corporate sector. These were expert in communications, not education. It proved to be a wise investment. Schools no longer felt isolated or abandoned. TLT was frequently in touch with them, and they knew who to contact. Everyone in the organization was approachable; there were no barriers to dialogue. The marketing team was highly active, with good news stories replacing the previous scandals in the local and national press. Hackney education was in the news but this time for positive reasons. This was part of celebration, which went hand-in-glove with communication to build confidence.

Celebration. The decision to make celebration a high priority came from early discussions between The Learning Trust and headteachers. Presenting awards such as teacher of the year was not part of the culture in English education back in 2002. People were reluctant to put themselves forward for such accolades and felt embarrassed if they were singled out for praise. That continues to some extent, but the national Teaching Awards Trust, headed by Lord Puttnam, broke the ice in 1998. Headteachers were conscious of the outstanding work that went unnoticed in Hackney schools and wanted TLT to do something about it. That was when the marketing team got involved. One of the outcomes was the annual Hackney education awards: one set for teachers and one for students. The combined effect of the awards that signal appreciation and the consistent publication of good news stories about Hackney schools in the local and national press created a huge confidence in Hackney that was shared by the community, everyone in the schools, and TLT. It created an upward spiral as people felt good about their work and themselves, which, in turn, ensured they continued to grow.

Estelle Morris paid tribute to the work of TLT in Hackney:

> Politicians don't teach children and they don't lead schools, so they are constantly looking for levers for improvement. The idea of The Learning Trust was a brand new lever, it was a new vehicle. The people who gave life to it in Hackney really did gather the best around them and did a first-class job. It's been such a good news story that we are at risk of forgetting how it was done. It wouldn't have happened without The Learning Trust and they deserve huge credit for bringing it all about.[33]

Having shown that schools in the poorest part of London can perform at the same level as anywhere else, Alan Wood concluded: "We have created a platform where there are no excuses now, absolutely none. Nobody can blame the local authority, or teachers or poor recruitment. Nobody can blame the kids. We've shown that schools in Hackney can do as well as schools anywhere."[34]

Tower Hamlets and Hackney Student Achievement, 2002–2012

We now analyze the student achievement data to review the outcomes of these reforms. We have presented these two cases as excellent examples of balancing and integrating push and pull factors. Thus we would expect them to show impressive results. We begin with secondary schools, as this was the main focus of London Challenge and the first priority in Hackney. Figure 4.3 shows the improvements in Hackney and Tower Hamlets compared with the national averages. It reveals the significant contribution these boroughs made to the improvements across Inner London shown in Figure 4.2.

There are 10 levels in the English national curriculum. Students are expected to reach Level 4 at age 11 (end of Key Stage 2). The performance across primary schools is shown in two charts because the government changed its benchmark after 2006. Up to then, the benchmark measure

Figure 4.3. Percentage of 16-Year-Old Students Achieving at Least Five GCSE Grades A*–C, Including English and Mathematics, for England, London, Hackney, and Tower Hamlets, 2004 to 2012

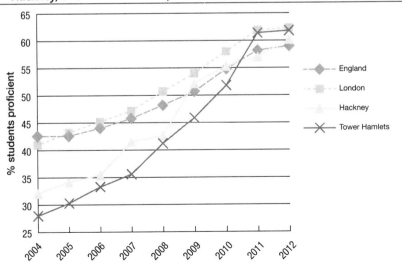

Figure 4.4. Aggregate of Percentages of Students at Level 4 or Higher in National Tests at End of Key Stage 2 (11-Year-Olds) for English, Mathematics, and Science in England, Hackney, and Tower Hamlets, from 1996 to 2006

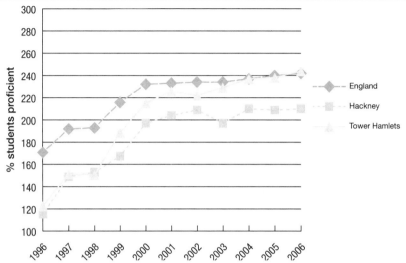

was the percentage of students achieving Level 4 or higher in the national tests for English, mathematics, and science. We show the aggregate of these three tests, out of 300, up to 2006.

Figure 4.4 shows the remarkable improvements in Tower Hamlets from 1998 onward. There was clearly something here above and beyond the national strategies. The gap between Tower Hamlets and the national average was closed by 2004. Meanwhile improvements in Hackney were in line with the national trend but not closing the gap. Given what we know about the lack of school support in Hackney up to 2002, this is not surprising. After TLT started to work in 2002 there was a dip. But results in Hackney remained flat until 2006. In this period TLT was firefighting and working on its Find & Fix just to keep pace with the national trend.

The government introduced two changes to the national tests around this time. In 2005 the benchmark changed and new performance level was the percentage of students who reached Level 4 or higher in *both* the English and the mathematics tests. After 2006 the science test was abandoned altogether.

Figure 4.5 shows improvements against the current benchmark. There is an overlap for 2005 and 2006 with Figure 4.4. Performance in Tower Hamlets is slightly better than the national averages over this 8-year period. It shows that the systemwide improvements were secure and schools

Figure 4.5. Percentage of Students at Level 4 or Higher in National Tests at End of Key Stage 2 for Both English and Mathematics in England, Hackney, and Tower Hamlets, from 2005 to 2012

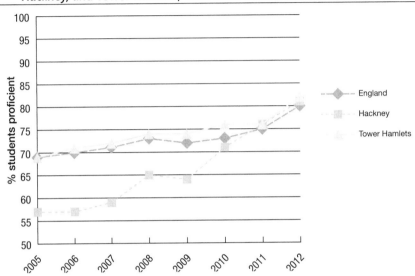

were sustaining their high performance. For Hackney, the data suggest that the longer-term strategies came to fruition after 2006 as the gap with the national average was gradually closed. The slight dip in 2009 mirrors a dip in the national results and is most likely a test issue. The surge in performance after 2009 is astonishing. Both Hackney and Tower Hamlets performed above the national average in 2011 and 2012.

We also analyzed the achievement gaps in England, London, Hackney, and Tower Hamlets for secondary and primary schools according to students' ethnicity, first language, family income, and special educational needs. Although we present the conclusions below, we do not report these data here; the detailed analysis is available in online Appendix C at www.tcpress.com.

In terms of ethnicity, the gap between the highest-performing group and the lowest has narrowed significantly from 2005 to 2012 for both 11-year-olds and 16-year-olds, across England, London, Hackney, and Tower Hamlets.

For students whose first language is not English, the gap between them and students whose mother tongue is English has been closed between 2006 and 2012 across England, London, and Hackney at ages 11 and 16. In Tower Hamlets, the students who speak English as an additional language outperform the native English speakers at both ages.

We compared results for children from low-income families with the rest. In 2006, on average, those in poverty performed at significantly lower levels. The gaps in secondary performances remain roughly the same although with much narrower gaps in Hackney and Tower Hamlets than England and London overall. In primary schools the gaps close slightly in England, London, and Hackney. Interestingly, in Tower Hamlets the GCSE (age 16) average for students from low-income families (59.4%) is above the overall national average for England (59%). This is compelling evidence that with the right support, children from low-income families can perform as well as the rest.

The performance of students with special educational needs in secondary schools has improved in line with the rest, but the gap has not been reduced. In primary schools the gap is slightly less by 2012, when across London over half the students with special needs achieve the benchmark of Level 4 in both English and mathematics.

CONCLUSION:
INTEGRATING PUSH AND PULL

The London case has several clear lessons for improving large systems that link to the framework we present in Chapter 1. First we see the broken-down reforms in the preceding decades that were too pushy and failed through implementation. Some of them were fine ideas; others just wouldn't work anyway. We see in this case desperate problems that were considered by many as impossible to solve. Then we see the evolution of leadership that starts to bring together a confluence of a small number of key factors with resolute leadership, a "no excuses" mind-set, and the generation and cultivation of capacity, confidence, and commitment to a level that breakthrough results are sustained, even in the most challenging districts of Tower Hamlets and Hackney. Two subtleties around the framework emerge in this case. First, to achieve balance, you don't always have to push and pull yourself; you can let someone else do the pushing while you get on with the pulling. This was the essential approach in London Challenge. Second, the push doesn't have to come from the top or the system leaders. We see in Tower Hamlets how competition between schools, where collaboration was a very strong feature, provided an edge that kept them moving forward—always doing better than before.

Most of all we see that it is possible over the period of a decade to take a system with rock-bottom morale and performance and transform it into a system of proud achievement with a commitment to continuous improvement. It required tremendous effort to become successful, but the effort was spread over many who worked together or in concert. It was hard work, but our guess was that it didn't feel like drudgery for those doing it, and that it almost certainly is not as hard as going to work in a failing system day after day. Whether the momentum will continue is another matter. It takes applying a great deal of attention and energy to continuous renewal in order to maintain the efforts we have just described, and we fear that the current education reform context in England may not be conducive to continued success on the scale we have seen in this chapter. But that story will be for another book in the future.

CHAPTER 5

Lessons Learned

A Matter of Integrated Balance

As we said in Chapter 1, big-city reform is, well, "big"—and complex, unpredictable, fused with politics and personalities. There are hundreds of references in Chapters 2–4 to evaluation reports, articles in journals, books, and newspapers that provide much more information to deepen your understanding of big-city reform. We could not include everything there is, but we have referred to enough for even the most voracious appetite. At this point we have to leave it to you to plan your own learning journeys and to follow up on issues of particular interest. In some ways these chapters form an encyclopedia of big-city reforms because so many different initiatives were tried with varying success. In this chapter we do offer concrete lessons, but our overall advice is that you understand your own context and be guided by what you discover and by your hope for the future. Although you can find useful ideas in the case stories, they will need to be adapted to suit your own situation. Every big city is unique and must be treated as such. On the other hand, we do think that the push–pull framework and the insights within its dynamics are instructive for all those interested in improving big education systems.

Our intention of analyzing these three big-city reforms over this busy decade was a hugely complex challenge. Most single reforms are complicated in themselves, but the immense volume of different initiatives across three big cities that carried on over 10 years was overwhelming. Our recourse was to employ the concept of *simplexity,* which we introduced in Chapter 1. By reducing the many different nuances to the least number of key factors that cut across the three cases, we were able to see the woods from the trees. We settled on six purposeful actions that were used time and again. We recognized a division between them. Some were bold, assertive actions that tend to *push* the reform through the system. By contrast, others were more invitational and attractive; they tended to *pull* and met less resistance. Of course these are oversimplified, but that is the point of *simplexity.* We are not saying that big-city reform can be reduced to a bullet list of six simple principles that, if applied, will guarantee successful reform. Instead, we offer it as a tool that may be used to explore big-city reforms, understand them better, and discover the nuances for yourself.

COMPARING PUSH–PULL ACTIONS FROM THE CASES

In New York City, Mayor Michael Bloomberg and his school chancellor Joel Klein were very pushy leaders—put positively, they challenged the status quo to put "children first." They were charged with reforming a stifling and corrupt bureaucracy with a ticking clock, as mayoral control was time-limited by the state. Children First was a powerful manifesto embodying this commitment. In London, Tower Hamlets had resolute leadership that kept them on track when the government itself was trying to blow them off course. And in Hackney the push came from the "ferocious assertion" that children in poverty could do as well as any other children, given the right support. Central leadership was not so evident in Toronto, but the combination of relentless insistence on changing the status quo at the provincial level and a spattering of local leaders who wanted change proved powerful as a signal for reform.

We found trusted leaders who succeeded in pulling people to them and working out commonly owned strategies. We saw this in London—Christine Gilbert, the director of Tower Hamlets; Sir Mike Tomlinson and Alan Wood of The Learning Trust in Hackney; and Sir Tim Brighouse of the London Challenge. In Ontario, the premier at the provincial level, the head of the Literacy and Numeracy Secretariat, and a second tier of leaders at TDSB served that role. New York City, by contrast, never had such trusted leadership in the decade in question. The leaders there forcefully challenged the status quo but never did build a constituency.

Hard, tough data were used as a challenge to drive through reforms. In London and Toronto these data systems were well established and well known by all in the system, for example, comparing schools with others like them, in "families of schools," and so on. By and large the data were seen to be reliable. NYC, on the other hand, had reams of data, but it was never clear how accurate they were and many debates ensued about their validity. The ARIS system was bogged down by delay, and it was difficult to navigate. In addition, the presence of varieties of data (city tests, state tests, NAEP assessments, and different ways of calculating graduation rates) often overwhelmed school-level leaders and confused the general public.

Resources were wisely invested to have the most direct impact on students' achievement. We saw this in Tower Hamlets and Hackney, where resources were directed with determination to foster professional learning, selection and cultivation of talent (human capital), and focused ways of helping and supporting groups to learn from one another in federations (use the group to change the group, or social capital and decisional capital). The same thing happened at TDSB, where a commitment (internal to the district), and a corresponding strategy for equity and excellence in student achievement, combined with an (external) provincial strategy to deepen instructional capacity building across a very large system.

The overall effect of the push and pull forces is captured in the cluster of outcomes we identified in Hackney: increased commitment, capacity, and confidence on the part of educators that carried them through unexpected challenges and enabled them to thrive when they worked together as breakthroughs occurred. In NYC there was a great deal of professional power unleashed by some of the strategies, but it was in pockets, not so accessible, and not sustainable as reorganizations occurred and leaders kept changing and moving in and out of clusters and the system as a whole. In other words, a great deal of professional capacity was unleashed, but it was hard for the system as a whole to access and leverage it.

To further illustrate our dynamic framework, in Figure 5.1 we draw push and pull examples from the three cases in Chapters 2–4.

SCORING BALANCE IN REFORM ACTIONS

What we learn from these cases of big-city reform is the essential equilibrium between push and pull purposeful actions. This, again, is part of *simplexity*. It is a very simple idea that you need to balance pushes and pulls. Try doing it. The simplest ideas are often very difficult to achieve. The difficulty stems from the complexity of the situation. And big cities are very complex systems. Not only that, they are constantly changing. You are not facing the same situation day after day. But if you are alert, sensitive to your environment, and responsive to it, you will have a better chance of success as long as you keep your nerve and strive to achieve balance in your purposeful actions.

Becoming a balanced leader with depth in both pull and push and their integration will mobilize others in the cause, and you will be surprised at how much energy educators will put into the effort. Professionals love a big challenge and a bigger platform for success. System leaders need to figure out how to take advantage of this natural proclivity and avoid the opposite—making a hard task even harder by not being a balanced leader.

As we consider a balance in reform actions for the three case cities, we could affix ratings to the three sets of connected dimensions of push and

Figure 5.1. Push and Pull Vignettes from New York City, London, and Toronto

PUSH ACTIONS	PULL ACTIONS
Challenge the status quo	**Create a commonly owned strategy**
Across London, and particularly in Hackney and Tower Hamlets, the acceptance that children from low-income homes could not pass their exams on time was vigorously challenged. Acknowledging that some schools had more problems than others, the expectation was that their students would perform at the same high levels as everyone else. No excuses were accepted. With additional resources, the system was able to accelerate learning of the neediest students, and the system topped the national averages.	In the early days of the Ontario Strategy there were deliberate actions to encourage innovation in schools across the district school boards by funding small projects. It indicated that the system wanted to learn in partnership with the profession. It demonstrated trust in teachers, who responded willingly because they had an opportunity to engage in shaping the reform. Outstanding work was published in *Schools on the Move* and a similar document for districts. It led to the Lighthouse Program and the rapid spread of good ideas from school to school without the pressure of mandates.
Convey a high sense of urgency (with data)	**Develop professional power of capital**
The accountability system developed by Jim Liebman in NYC did this particularly well using three different kinds of data, rather than relying solely on test scores. First, it combined quantitative data about individual students' progress with their overall achievement in the school's Progress Report. Second, the Quality Review formed qualitative judgments about schools based on self-evaluation and external review. And third, students, teachers, and parents were surveyed annually to collect their views about the school. The system was deliberately designed to provide schools with a wide range of data to use for improvement planning.	The Aspiring Principals Program developed by Sandra Stein at the NYC Leadership Academy is a fine example. It provides a 6-week intensive summer school that simulates the kind of challenges candidates will face in schools. That is followed by a 10-month school-based residency with an experienced principal as mentor. Candidates must pass rigorous performance standards in order to graduate. The program is led by former successful NYC principals. Graduates must commit to serving in NYC schools for at least 5 years. By 2012, one in six principals across the city had graduated from the Aspiring Principals Program.

PUSH ACTIONS	PULL ACTIONS
Have the courage to intervene	**Attend to sustainability**
The Keys to Success program introduced by the London Challenge is an example of having the courage to intervene in the most persistently failing schools. These were the schools with stubbornly low exam results and a long list of problems from low morale to teacher shortages. Advisers worked with the schools and brokered extra support for them. But the schools had to work out what they wanted themselves. Rather than provide the money to the schools, London Challenge paid for the support directly. Each school developed its own unique way of breaking the link between poverty and low achievement.	A good example of sustainable improvement is through collaborative inquiry, now developed widely across families of schools in Toronto. Teachers working in small teams select a group of low-performing students they teach. They rigorously analyze their students' assessments to find ways of helping them make better progress in learning. Through discussion, the teachers plan changes in their classroom practice or introduce new ideas, which they evaluate with peer review. They are always seeking ideas that will help the whole school improve, as well as their own class. The TDSB's long-standing commitment to stressing and supporting diagnosis-linked capacity-building action built the professional capital in deep pockets of the district.

pull, say by using a 10-point scale. This is a gross oversimplification, so do not treat the scores literally; they are notional in trying to capture the relative emphases. Our rough-and-ready estimates are the following:

New York City

- High on challenge (8 on the 10-point scale), medium on the use of accurate data (5), and high on courage to intervene (8)—for a total push score of 21 out of 30.
- On the pull dimension we see weakness on "commonly held vision" (5), uneven professional power (5), and weak conditions for sustainability (2)—for a pull total of 12 of 30.
Overall score: 33 out of 60.

Toronto

- Not quite the assertive push, but definitely strong and persistent: (7) for challenge, (8) for urgent use of data, and (7) for courage to intervene—total 22.
- We rate pull as stronger at (8), (9), and (8), as that was the main basis of the Ontario/Toronto strategy—total 25.
Overall score: 47 out of 60.

London (Tower Hamlets, Hackney)

- Three (8)s on the push factors, as there was resolute, relentless press for reform—24.
- On pull, strong common strategy formed (8), superb professional power (9), and strong conditions for sustainability (8)—for a total of 25.

Overall score: 49 out of 60.

Rather than a simple total score, the balance that we are seeking is better revealed in the radar chart shown in Figure 5.2. We see here that the forces for effective change are more an integrated interplay than a static balance of the six core factors. In this chart, the top three points are push actions, with their balancing pulls on the opposite end of each axis. The shape of the graph gives a visual representation of the overall balance of the reforms and conveys the *simplexity*. These are rough estimates and we do not intend that they be taken literally.

Referring to Figure 5.2, it is clear that in New York City the new mayor Bill de Blasio and his chancellor will have to virtually start from scratch, as there is almost no sustainability from the last decade of strategies. The good news is that there are considerable pockets of capacity and professional power that exist in the schools and clusters, and probably substantial pent-up moral imperative commitments *if* the system can shift its strategies toward the pull factors buttressed by the sense of urgency for

Figure 5.2. Push–Pull Purposeful Actions Evident in Big-City Reforms Across New York City, London, and Toronto, from 2002–2012

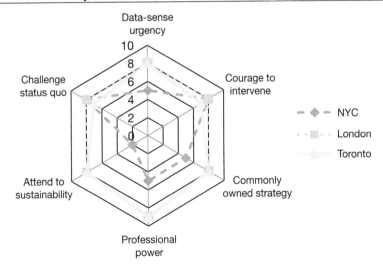

citywide improvement. We believe that there is considerable potential—a latent appetite, if you will—for NYC to take off in this next period under the right leadership, which would integrate the push and pull forces for "raising the bar and closing the gap" in student learning.

LOOKING AHEAD AT SYSTEM REFORM

Overall, our conclusion is that the 2014–2024 decade could be positively different. We have the cumulative knowledge and experience of digging deeply into system improvement over the last period with several clear do and don't lessons. For example, we see a shift in the United States, just emerging, where more and more leaders at the state and federal levels are realizing the limits of what we have called the "wrong drivers" (see as an indicator the July 14 editorial in the Sunday *New York Times* "The Trouble with the Testing Mania"[1]). We can also see big shifts in California, where we and others are working, as the governor, state superintendent, school districts and boards, and the California Teachers Association are forming new partnerships for whole-system change.

On the other hand, the forces favoring counterproductive push factors are considerable: negative accountability, isolated school autonomy, the continued deterioration of the teaching profession, mechanical instructional supervision, and layered-on technology. Push factors have a tendency to be more blatant, while pull ones stay underdeveloped. We need to reverse this tendency.

We have not attempted to address the future, and there is much else to consider. For example, we are currently deeply engaged in helping to integrate technology, pedagogy, and change knowledge in a way that could radically improve learning.[2] The six push and pull factors furnish a framework to tackle the change agenda of the immediate future. The years of 2002–2012 were indeed a busy decade for big-city education reform. Moreover, it was the first time that deliberate, transparent, well-documented strategies were put in action on a citywide basis. We are all better off for what we have learned from these leaders and cases. Now the task is to put this knowledge to work, learn by purposely doing, and accomplish results on a scale never before seen. We are better equipped for this journey because of efforts in New York City, Toronto, and London.

The next decade has already started—2014 will be the start of a new era in big-city school change. It is time to go for it with all the pull and push sophistication you can muster. Let's learn from the good history from the last decade, jettison the bad, and create a brand-new future history that will serve our urban dwellers well!

Notes

Preface

1. To find out more about *simplexity*, watch Eric Berlow at his TED talk (www.youtube.com/watch?v=_xI_4zYZ0JE) or read Kluger, J. (2008), *Simplexity: Why Simple Things Become Complicated.* New York, NY: Hyperion

Chapter 1: Tackling the Challenges of Urban Education

1. Data about world population trends are published by the United Nations Population Fund on their website, www.unfpa.org/pds/urbanization.htm

2. A conceptual framework was developed and published by the Organization for Economic Cooperation and Development (OECD) in 2007: *No more failures: Ten steps to equity in education* (Paris, France: OECD). A later report, published in 2012, *Equity and quality in education: Supporting disadvantaged students and schools* (Paris, France: OECD), gives evidence of policy levers that can help overcome school failure and reduce inequalities in OECD school systems. Additional information is available on the OECD website, www.oecd.org/education/school/overcomingschoolfailurepoliciesthatwork.htm

3. OECD, *No more failures.*

4. Wilkinson, R., & Pickett, K. (2009), *The spirit level: Why equality is better for everyone* (London, England: Penguin Books).

5. Jenkins, S. P., & Micklewright, J. (Eds.) (2007), *Inequality and poverty re-examined* (Oxford, England: Oxford University Press).

6. United Nations Children's Fund (UNICEF) (2013), *A post-2015 world fit for children: Sustainable development starts and ends with safe, healthy and well-educated children* (New York, NY: UNICEF).

7. Dynarski, M., & Gleason, P. (2002), How can we help? What we have learned from recent federal dropout prevention evaluations. *Journal for Education of Students Placed at Risk, 7,* 43–69.

8. For "resilience," see Maston, A. S. (2009), Ordinary magic: Lessons from research on resilience in human development. *Education Canada, 49*(3), 28–32; Ungar, M. (Ed.) (2005), *Handbook for working with children and youth: Pathways to resilience across cultures and contexts* (Thousand Oaks, CA: Sage).

For "social capital," see Putnam, R. (2000), *Bowling alone: The collapse and revival of American community* (New York, NY: Simon & Schuster); Woolcock, N., &

Narayan, D. (2000), Social capital: Implications for development theory, research and policy. *World Bank Research Observer, 15*(2): 225–249.

9. Raffo, C., Dyson, A., Gunter, H. M., Hall, D., Jones, L., & Kalambouka, A. (2010), *Education and poverty in affluent countries,* Routledge Research in Education (New York, NY: Routledge).

10. See Lloyd-Ellis, H. (2003), On the impacts of inequality on growth in the short and long run: A synthesis. *Canadian Public Policy, 29,* (Suppl. 1): S65–S86; Green, A., Preston J., & Janmaat, J. G. (2006), *Education, equality and social cohesion* (New York, NY: Palgrave Macmillan).

11. Joshee, R. (2004), Citizenship and multicultural education in Canada: From assimilation to social cohesion, *in* Banks, J. A. (Ed.), *Diversity and citizenship education: Global perspectives* (pp. 127–156) (San Francisco, CA: Jossey-Bass).

12. OECD (1996), *Lifelong learning for all* (Paris, France: OECD). This book is no longer in print, but the development of ideas has continued and may be followed on the OECD website, www.oecdobserver.org/news/archivestory.php/aid/432/Lifelong_learning_for_all.html

13. Sahlberg, P. (2011), *Finnish lessons: What can the world learn from educational change in Finland?* (New York, NY: Teachers College Press).

14. O'Connor, A. (2002), *Poverty knowledge: Social science, social policy and the poor in twentieth-century U.S. history* (Princeton, NJ: Princeton University Press), p. 5.

15. Educational inequity comes in many shapes and forms. These three texts cover some key issues: Rothstein, R. (2004), *Class and schools: Using social, economic and educational reform to close the black–white achievement gap* (New York, NY: Economic Policy Institute, Teachers College, Columbia University); Willms, J. D. (2002), *Vulnerable children: Findings from Canada's National Longitudinal Study of Children and Youth* (Edmonton, Canada: University of Alberta Press); Mortimore, P., & Whitty, G. (2000), *Can school improvement overcome the effects of disadvantage?,* Perspectives on Education Policy (London, England: Institute of Education, University of London).

16. There are many commentators on this issue. The following three are very pertinent to big-city reforms: Darling-Hammond, L. (2010), *The flat world and education: How America's commitment to equity will determine our future* (New York, NY: Teachers College Press); Ravitch, D. (2010), *The death and life of the great American school system: How testing and choice are undermining education* (New York, NY: Basic Books); Payne, C. M. (2008), *So much reform, so little change: The persistence of failure in urban schools* (Cambridge, MA: Harvard Educational Publishing Group).

17. Darling-Hammond, *The flat world and education;* Ravitch, *The death and life of the great American school system;* Payne, *So much reform, so little change.*

18. Sarason, S. B. (1971), *The culture of the school and the problem of change* (Boston, MA: Allyn & Bacon).

19. Fullan, M. (2011*), Choosing the wrong drivers for whole system reform* (Melbourne, Australia: Centre for Strategic Education).

20. Hargreaves, A., & Fullan, M. (2012), *Professional capital: Transforming teaching in every school* (New York, NY: Teachers College Press).

21. Kirtman, L. (2013), *Leadership and teams: The missing piece of the education reform puzzle* (London, England: Pearson).

22. By "failing school," we refer to schools whose students make significantly less progress than students in other schools with a similar intake of students.

23. Source of statistics: National Center for Educational Statistics, as presented in the figure entitled "Elementary and Secondary Education Funding: Fiscal Year 2010" *in* New America Foundation (2013, June 30), *Federal education budget project: Background &analysis: School finance,* retrieved from febp.newamerica.net/background-analysis/school-finance

24. Primary sources of achievement and financial data for NYC are: NYC Department of Education, New York State Board of Regents, and U.S. Department of Education. For Toronto: Ontario Ministry of Education and the Education Quality and Accountability Office for Ontario; graduation rates were collected from the Auditor General's annual reports. For London: UK Government Department for Education.

Chapter 2: New York City

1. United States Census Bureau (2013, June), *State & county quickfacts: New York (city), New York,* retrieved from quickfacts.census.gov/qfd/states/36/3651000.html

2. Barry, D. (1999, April 23), Raze School System, Giuliani Says. *New York Times,* retrieved from www.nytimes.com/1999/04/23/nyregion/raze-school-system-giuliani-says.html

3. For an account of the decentralization of the school system in 1969, see Ravitch, D. (2000), *The great school wars: a history of the New York City Public Schools* (Baltimore, MD: Johns Hopkins University Press).

4. Fruchter, N. (2008), 'Plus ça change . . .' : Mayoral control in New York City, *in* Boyd, W. L., Kerchner, C. T., & Blyth, M. (Eds.), *The transformation of great American school districts: How big cities are reshaping public education* (pp. 85–112) (Cambridge, MA: Harvard Education Press).

5. Levine, A. (2000, January 8), Make Giuliani the education mayor. *New York Times,* retrieved from www.nytimes.com/2000/01/08/opinion/make-giuliani-the-education-mayor.html

6. New York City Council, Committee on Education (2002, March 1), Meeting minutes (New York, NY: New York City Council), pp. 9–12, retrieved from legistar.council.nyc.gov/DepartmentDetail.aspx?ID=6903&GUID=5D939F6A-A26A-456C-BF68-2FE3903139C8&Search=

7. New York City Council, Committee on Education (2002, March 1), Meeting minutes, pp. 92–95.

8. New York City Council, Committee on Education (2002, March 19), Meeting minutes (New York, NY: New York City Council), retrieved from legistar.council.nyc.gov/DepartmentDetail.aspx?ID=6903&GUID=5D939F6A-A26A-456C-BF68-2FE3903139C8&Search=

9. Domanico, R. (2002, March), *State of New York City Public Schools 2002,* Civic Report No. 26 (New York, NY: Center for Civic Innovation, Manhattan Institute).

10. Domanico, *State of New York City Public Schools 2002.*

11. McDonald, J. P. (2009, April), *Autonomy and accountability in New York City reform,* paper presented at the annual meeting of the American Educational Research Association, San Diego, CA

12. Fliegel, S., with MacGuire, J. (1993), *Miracle in East Harlem: The fight for choice in public education* (New York, NY: Times Books/Random House).

13. Meier, D. (2002), *The power of their ideas: Lessons from a small school in Harlem* (New York, NY: Beacon Press).

14. Elmore, R., & Burney, D. (1998), *Continuous improvement in community district #2, New York City* (Pittsburgh, PA: High Performance Learning Communities Project, Learning Research and Development Center, University of Pittsburgh).

15. Darling-Hammond, L., Ancess, J., & Ort, S. W. (2002), Reinventing high school: Outcomes of the Coalition Campus Schools Projects. *American Educational Research Journal, 39*(3), 639–673.

16. Institute for Education and Social Policy (2001), *Final report of the evaluation of the New York Networks for School Renewal, 1996–2001* (NYU Steinhardt, NY: Institute for Education and Social Policy).

17. Foley, E. M., Klinge, A., & Reisner, E. R. (2007), *Evaluation of New Century high schools: Profile of an initiative to create and sustain small, successful high schools* (Washington, DC: Policy Studies Associates).

18. NYC Department of Education (2013), *About us: Panel for educational policy,* retrieved from schools.nyc.gov/AboutUs/leadership/PEP/default.htm

19. Gendar, A., & Saltonstall, D. (2002, July 30), Lawyer picked as chancellor. *New York Daily News,* retrieved from www.nydailynews.com/archives/news/lawyer-picked-chancellor-joel-klein-federal-business-background-article-1.510626

20. Childress, S., Higgins, M., Ishimaru, A., & Takahashi, S. (2011). Managing for results at the New York Department of Education, *in* O'Day, J., Bitter, C. S., & Gomez, L. M. (Eds.), *Education reform in New York City: Ambitious change in the nation's most complex school system* (pp. 87–108) (Cambridge, MA: Harvard Education Press), p. 89.

21. Hill, P. T. (2011). Leadership and governance in New York City reform, *in* O'Day et al., *Education reform in New York City* (pp. 17–32), p. 21.

22. Williams, J. (2003, September 2), School bells to ring in big changes, *New York Daily News,* retrieved from www.nydailynews.com/archives/news/school-bells-ring-big-new-curriculum-tests-schedules-districts-article-1.527154

23. Herszenhorn, D. (2004, March 25), Not so long out of school, yet running the system. *New York Times,* retrieved from www.nytimes.com/2004/03/25/education/25educrats.html

24. O'Day, J., & Bitter, C. J. (2011), Improving instruction in New York City, *in* O'Day et al., *Education reform in New York City* (pp. 109–130), p. 113.

25. Lewin, T. (2002, August 31), Educator has accomplishments and enemies. *New York Times,* retrieved from www.nytimes.com/2002/08/31/nyregion/educator-has-accomplishments-and-enemies.html?pagewanted=all&src=pm

26. Traub, J. (2003, August 3), New York's new approach. *New York Times,* retrieved from www.nytimes.com/2003/08/03/education/new-york-s-new-approach.html ?pagewanted=all&src=pm

27. Ravitch, D. (2010), *The death and life of the great American school system: How testing and choice are undermining education* (New York, NY: Basic Books), p. 73.

28. Herszenhorn, D. (2004, March 11), Former Deputy Chancellor blames dismissal on politics. *New York Times,* retrieved from www.nytimes.com/2004/03/11/ nyregion/former-deputy-chancellor-blames-dismissal-on-politics.html

29. Ravitch, *Death and life of the great American school system,* p. 79.

30. Herszenhorn, D. (2004, March 16), Bloomberg wins on school tests after firing foes. *New York Times,* retrieved from www.nytimes.com/2004/03/16/nyregion/ bloomberg-wins-on-school-tests-after-firing-foes.html?pagewanted=all&src=pm

31. Childress et al., Managing for results at the New York Department of Education, pp. 89–90.

32. Coalition of Essential Schools (2005), *Horace talks with Eric Nadelstern: New York City's Autonomy Zone,* retrieved from www.essentialschools.org/resources/312

33. Herszenhorn, D. (2005, October 3), City and teachers union reach tentative accord on contract. *New York Times,* retrieved from www.nytimes.com/2005/10/03/ nyregion/03cnd-teach.html?pagewanted=all&_r=0

34. Herszenhorn, D. (2006, January 20), Schools chancellor says new overhaul will give more principals more autonomy. *New York Times.* Retrieved from www. nytimes.com/2006/01/20/nyregion/20schools.html

35. Chancellor Klein, quoted in Herszenhorn, Schools chancellor says new overhaul will give more principals more autonomy.

36. Coalition of Essential Schools, *Horace talks with Eric Nadelstern.*

37. New York City Council, Committee on Education (2007, March 5), Meeting minutes (New York, NY: New York City Council), retrieved from legistar. council.nyc.gov/DepartmentDetail.aspx?ID=6903&GUID=5D939F6A-A26A -456C-BF68-2FE3903139C8&Search=

38. New York City Council, Committee on Education (2007, March 5), Meeting minutes.

39. New York City Department of Education (2008–2009), *Children first: A bold, common-sense plan to create great schools for all New York City children* (New York, NY: NYC Department of Education), retrieved from schools.nyc.gov/NR/ rdonlyres/51C61E8F-1AE9-4D37-8881-4D688D4F843A/0/cf_corenarrative.pdf

40. Herszenhorn, D. (2007, April 17), Klein specifies restructuring of city schools. *New York Times,* retrieved from www.nytimes.com/2007/04/17/nyregion /17schools.html

41. Cuban, L. (2013), *Inside the black box of classroom practice: Change without reform in American education* (Cambridge, MA: Harvard Education Press).

42. Childress et al., Managing for results at the New York Department of Education, p. 92.

43. Gootman, E. (2006, April 12), Principals face review in education overhaul. *New York Times,* retrieved from www.nytimes.com/2006/04/12/education/12klein.

html?pagewanted=all. See also Chancellor Klein's press release: NYC Department of Education (2006, April 11), Schools Chancellor Joel I. Klein announces launch of accountability initiative, retrieved from schools.nyc.gov/Offices/mediarelations/NewsandSpeeches/2005-2006/04112006pressrelease.htm

44. Childress et al., Managing for results at the New York Department of Education, pp. 94–100.

45. See Glatter, R., Woods, P. A., & Bagley, C. (Eds.) (1997), *Choice and diversity in schooling: Perspectives and prospects* (London, England: Routledge); Scott, J. (Ed.) (2005), *School choice and diversity: What the evidence says* (New York, NY: Teachers College Press).

46. Herszenhorn, D. (2005, September 10), $250 million city program to promote charter schools. *New York Times,* retrieved from www.nytimes.com/2005/09/10/nyregion/10charter.html

47. See Foley et al., *Evaluation of New Century high schools*

48. See Fliegel with MacGuire, *Miracle in East Harlem*

49. For a history of choice in NYC schools and an account of NYC high schools' admissions process, see Corcoran, S. P., & Levin, H. M. (2011), School choice and competition in the New York City schools, *in* O'Day et al., *Education reform in New York City* (pp. 199–224).

50. Herszenhorn, D. (2003, September 18), Gates charity gives $51 million to city to start 67 schools. *New York Times,* retrieved from www.nytimes.com/2003/09/18/nyregion/gates-charity-gives-51-million-to-city-to-start-67-schools.html?src=pm

51. Quint, J. C., Smith, J. K., Unterman, R., & Moedano, A. E. (2010), *New York City's Changing High School Landscape: High Schools and Their Characteristics 2002–2008* (New York, NY: MDRC).

52. Quint et al., *New York City's Changing High School Landscape.*

53. Bloom, H. S., Levy Thomson, S., & Unterman, R. (2010), *Transforming high school experience: How New York City's small high schools are boosting student achievement and graduation rates* (New York, NY: MDRC).

54. Bloom, H. S., & Unterman, R. (2012), *Sustained positive effects on graduation rates produced by New York City's small public high schools of choice* (New York: MDRC).

55. Hemphill, C., & Nauer, K. (2009), *The new market place: How small school reforms and school choice have reshaped New York City's high schools* (New York: Center for New York City Affairs), pp. 16–17, retrieved from www.newschool.edu/milano/nycaffairs/publications_schools_thenewmarketplace.aspx

56. Ravitch, *Death and life of the great American school system,* p.84.

57. Herszenhorn, D. (2005, January 14), In push for small schools, other schools suffer. *New York Times,* retrieved from www.nytimes.com/2005/01/14/nyregion/14school.html?_r=0

58. Hemphill & Nauer, *The new market place,* pp. 35–42.

59. Chancellor Klein, quoted in Hemphill & Nauer, *The new market place,* p. 40.

60. New York City Working Group on School Transformation (2012), *The way forward from sanctions to supports* (Providence, RI: Annenberg Institute for School

Reform at Brown University), retrieved from annenberginstitute.org/publication/way-forward-sanctions-supports

61. Hemphill & Nauer, *The new market place,* p. 22.

62. Jennings, J. L., & Pallas, A. M. (2010), *Do New York City's new small schools enroll students with different characteristics from other NYC schools?* (Providence, RI: Annenberg Institute for School Reform at Brown University), p. 7.

63. Weinstein, M. G., Jacobowitz, R., Maguire, C., Saunders, T. B., & Fruchter, N. (2007), *Stability in student and teacher characteristics in the first ten years: A study of small high schools in New York City* (New York, NY: Institute for Education and Social Policy, New York University).

64. Fruchter, N., Hester, M., Mokhtar, C., & Shahn, Z. (2012), *Is demography still destiny? Neighborhood demographics and public high school students' readiness for college in New York City* (Providence, RI: Annenberg Institute for School Reform at Brown University).

65. Holzman, M. (2011), *A rotting apple: Education redlining in New York City* (Cambridge, MA: Schott Foundation for Public Education).

66. Jennings & Pallas, *Do New York City's new small schools enroll students,* pp. 12–18.

67. NYC Department of Education (2013), *Periodic assessments,* retrieved from schools.nyc.gov/Accountability/resources/assessments/PAOptions.htm

68. NYC Department of Education (2013), ARIS and ARIS parent link, retrieved from schools.nyc.gov/Accountability/resources/aris/ARIS.htm#whatisaris

69. Colvin, J., & Zimmer, A. (2012, July 30), City's $80M student data system to be replaced by state portal. *DNAinfo.com New York,* retrieved from www.dnainfo.com/new-york/20120730/new-york-city/citys-80m-student-data-system-be-replaced-by-state-portal

70. NYC Department of Education (2013), Children First Intensive, retrieved from schools.nyc.gov/Accountability/resources/childrenfirst/default.htm

71. Talbert, J. E. (2011), Collaborative inquiry to expand student success in New York City schools, *in* O'Day et al., *Education reform in New York City* (pp. 131–155).

72. Talbert, Collaborative inquiry to expand student success, p. 137.

73. Robinson, M., Kannapel, P., Gujarati, J., Williams, H., & Oettenger, A. (2008), *Formative study of the implementation of the inquiry team process in New York City Public Schools: 2007–2008 findings* (New York, NY: Columbia University, Teachers College, Consortium for Policy Research in Education) retrieved from www.cpre.org/formative-study-implementation-inquiry-team-process-new-york-city-public-schools-2007-08-findings

74. Robinson, M. A. (2010), *School perspectives on collaborative inquiry: Lessons learned from New York City 2009–2010* (New York, NY: Columbia University, Teachers College, Consortium for Policy Research in Education), retrieved from www.cpre.org/images/stories/cpre_pdfs/ci-llreport2010final%28nov%29.pdf

75. Talbert, Collaborative inquiry to expand student success, pp. 131–135, 143.

76. Tucker, B. (2010), *Putting data into practice: Lessons from New York City* (Washington, DC: Education Sector Reports), pp. 12–13, retrieved from www. educationsector.org/publications/putting-data-practice

77. Goertz, M., Loeb, S., & Wycoff, W. (2011), Recruiting, evaluating and retaining teachers: The Children First strategy to improve New York City's teachers, *in* O'Day et al., *Education reform in New York City* (pp. 157–177).

78. Goertz et al., Recruiting, evaluating and retaining teachers, p. 159.

79. Boyd, D., Lankford, H., Loeb, S., Rockoff, J., & Wycoff, J. (2008), The narrowing gap in New York City teacher qualifications and its implications for student achievement in high poverty schools. *Journal of Policy Analysis and Management, 27*(4), 793–818.

80. Goertz et al., Recruiting, evaluating and retaining teachers, pp. 160–163.

81. Kane, T. J., Rockoff, J. E., & Staiger, D. O. (2008), What does certification tell us about teacher effectiveness? Evidence from New York City. *Economics of Education Review, 27*, 615–631.

82. Boyd et. al., The narrowing gap in New York City teacher qualifications.

83. Goertz et al., Recruiting, evaluating and retaining teachers, p. 171.

84. See the website of NYC Leadership Academy, www.nycleadershipacademy. org/

85. Corcoran, S. P., Schwartz, A. E., & Weinstein, M. (2009), *The New York City aspiring principals program: A school-level evaluation* (New York, NY: Institute for Education and Social Policy, New York University), retrieved from www. wallacefoundation.org/knowledge-center/school-leadership/principal-evaluation /Documents/New-York-City-Aspiring-Principals-Program.pdf

86. Fullan, M. (2014), *The principal: Three keys for maximizing impact* (Hoboken, NJ: Wiley).

87. Chan, S. (2007, October 17), Mayor announces plan for teacher merit pay. *New York Times,* retrieved from cityroom.blogs.nytimes.com/2007/10/17/ mayor-announces-plan-for-teacher-merit-pay/

88. Marsh, J. A., Springer, M. G., McCaffrey, D. F., Yuan, K., Epstein, S., Koppich, J., . . . Peng, A. (2011), *A big apple for educators: New York City's experiment with school-wide performance bonuses* (Santa Monica, CA: RAND Corporation).

89. Otterman, S. (2011, July 17), New York City abandons teacher bonus program. *New York Times,* retrieved from www.nytimes.com/2011/07/18/education /18rand.html

90. Goertz et al., Recruiting, evaluating and retaining teachers, p. 175.

91. Ravitch, D., & Weingarten, R. (2004, March 18), Public schools, minus the public. *New York Times,* retrieved from www.nytimes.com/2004/03/18/opinion/ public-schools-minus-the-public.html

92. Henig, J. R., Gold, E., Orr, M., Silander, M., & Simon, E. (2011), Parent and community engagement in New York City and the sustainability challenge for urban education reform, *in* O'Day et al., *Education reform in New York City* (pp. 33–54), p. 39.

93. Santos, F., & Otterman, S. (2011, March 18), School-liaison office is accused of pushing a political cause. *New York Times,* retrieved from www.nytimes.com/2011/03/19/nyregion/19family.html?pagewanted=all

94. Henig et al., Parent and community engagement in New York City, p. 42.

95. Thompson, W. C., Jr. (2009), *Powerless parents: How the New York City Department of Education blocks parental influence in local school governance,* Policy Report (New York, NY: Office of the New York City Comptroller).

96. Barbaro, M., & Chen, D. W. (2008, October 1), Bloomberg expected to seek his third term as mayor. *New York Times,* retrieved from www.nytimes.com/2008/10/01/nyregion/01bloomberg.html?pagewanted=all

97. Medina, J. (2009, August 7), N.Y. Senate renews mayor's power to run schools. *New York Times,* retrieved from www.nytimes.com/2009/08/07/nyregion/07control.html

98. Barbaro, M., & Chen, D. W. (2009, November 4), Bloomberg wins 3rd term as mayor in unexpectedly close race. *New York Times,* retrieved from www.nytimes.com/2009/11/04/nyregion/04mayor.html?pagewanted=all; Barbaro, M. (2009, November 27), Bloomberg spent $102 million to win 3rd term. *New York Times,* retrieved from cityroom.blogs.nytimes.com/2009/11/27/bloomberg-spent-102-million-to-win-3rd-term/

99. Henig et al., Parent and community engagement in New York City, p. 51.

100. Otterman, S., & Medina, J. (2010, January 27), Boos and personal attacks as city panel prepares to vote on school closures. *New York Times,* retrieved from www.nytimes.com/2010/01/27/education/27closings.html

101. Otterman, S. (2010, March 26), Judge blocks closing of 19 New York City schools. *New York Times,* retrieved from www.nytimes.com/2010/03/27/nyregion/27close.html

102. Otterman, S. (2010, May 18), Uncertain future for a school in limbo. *New York Times,* retrieved from cityroom.blogs.nytimes.com/2010/05/18/uncertain-future-for-a-school-already-in-limbo/

103. Otterman, S. (2010, June 25), Bracing for 35 probable school closings next year. *New York Times,* retrieved from cityroom.blogs.nytimes.com/2010/06/25/bracing-for-35-likely-school-closings-next-year/

104. Medina, J. (2010, July 1), Court says city must keep struggling schools open. *New York Times,* retrieved from cityroom.blogs.nytimes.com/2010/07/01/court-says-city-must-keep-poorly-performing-schools-open/

105. Otterman, S. (2010, October 28), City considering 47 schools for closing. *New York Times,* retrieved from cityroom.blogs.nytimes.com/2010/10/28/city-considering-47-schools-for-closing/

106. Green, E. (2009, March 10), A DOE plan to personalize bureaucracy is making unions nervous. *Gotham Schools,* retrieved from gothamschools.org/2009/03/10/a-doe-plan-to-personalize-bureaucracy-is-making-unions-nervous/

107. A description of the school support networks may be found on the NYC Department of Education website: schools.nyc.gov/AboutUs/schools/support/default.htm

108. NYC Department of Education (2013), *Community and high school superintendents*, retrieved from schools.nyc.gov/AboutUs/schools/superintendents/default.htm

109. Medina, J. (2010, April 26), In shake-up, principals may get more say in what is taught. *New York Times,* retrieved from www.nytimes.com/2010/04/27/nyregion/27tweed.html

110. Otterman, S. (2010, November 29), With deal, Bloomberg's pick wins helm of city schools. *New York Times,* retrieved from www.nytimes.com/2010/11/30/nyregion/30waiver.html?pagewanted=all

111. Chen, D. W., & Barbaro, W. (2010, November 10), Bloomberg took secret path to a new schools chief. *New York Times,* retrieved from www.nytimes.com/2010/11/11/nyregion/11search.html

112. Santos, F. (2010, December 13), New schools no. 2 wants more and better testing. *New York Times,* retrieved from www.nytimes.com/2010/12/14/nyregion/14deputy.html?pagewanted=all

113. Santos, F. (2011, January 21), A top overseer of city schools plans to retire. *New York Times,* retrieved from www.nytimes.com/2011/01/22/nyregion/22deputy.html

114. Otterman, S. (2011, February 3), Protesting school closings in an annual noisy ritual. *New York Times,* retrieved from: www.nytimes.com/2011/02/04/nyregion/04panel.html

115. Winerip, M. (2011, February 4), In panel's votes to close low-performing schools, rage and foregone decisions. *New York Times,* retrieved from www.nytimes.com/2011/02/05/nyregion/05winerip.html

116. Otterman, S. (2011, April 4), Experienced, homegrown educator leaves city schools. *New York Times,* retrieved from cityroom.blogs.nytimes.com/2011/04/04/experienced-homegrown-educator-leaves-city-schools/

117. Gootman, E., & Barbaro, M.. (2011, April 7), Cathleen Black is out as city schools chancellor. *New York Times,* retrieved from cityroom.blogs.nytimes.com/2011/04/07/cathie-black-is-out-as-chancellor/

118. Chen, D. W. (2011, May 11), Bloomberg given poor marks in new poll. *New York Times,* retrieved from cityroom.blogs.nytimes.com/2011/05/11/bloomberg-given-poor-marks-in-new-poll/

119. Kaplan, T. (2011, April 12), A far different Albany debut for this schools chief. *New York Times,* retrieved from cityroom.blogs.nytimes.com/2011/04/12/a-far-different-albany-debut-for-this-schools-chief/

120. Halbfinger, D. M., Hernandez, J. C., & Santos, F. (2011, April 23), In New York's schools chief, a knack for quiet conciliation. *New York Times,* retrieved from www.nytimes.com/2011/04/24/nyregion/dennis-walcott-brings-softer-touch-to-chancellor-role.html?pagewanted=all

121. Santos, F. (2011, September 7), A gentler touch atop the schools, after years of a hard push for reform. *New York Times,* retrieved from www.nytimes.com/2011/09/08/nyregion/chancellor-dennis-m-walcott-wants-civility-and-progress-in-city-schools.html

122. NYC Department of Education (2011, July 15), *Agreement Between Department of Education and Teachers' Union Will Help Secure $65 Million in Federal Funds for Struggling Schools,* retrieved from schools.nyc.gov/Offices/mediarelations/NewsandSpeeches/2011-2012/fedfundsagreement071511.htm

123. Chen, D. W., & Phillips, A. W. (2012, January 12), Mayor takes on teachers' union in school plans. *New York Times,* retrieved from www.nytimes.com/2012/01/13/nyregion/in-state-of-the-city-speech-bloomberg-focuses-on-schools.html

124. Medina, J. (2008, October 8), Teachers to be measured based on students' standardized test scores. *New York Times,* retrieved from www.nytimes.com/2008/10/02/education/02teachers.html?pagewanted=all

125. Medina, J. (2008, March 18), Bill would bar linking class test scores to tenure. *New York Times,* retrieved from www.nytimes.com/2008/03/18/nyregion/18teacher.html

126. Medina, J. (2009, September 9), 12,000 teacher data reports but what to do? *New York Times,* retrieved from www.nytimes.com/2009/09/09/nyregion/09teachers.html

127. Medina, J. (2009, November 26), Mayor says student test scores will factor into teacher tenure. *New York Times,* retrieved from www.nytimes.com/2009/11/26/education/26teachers.html?pagewanted=all

128. Medina, J. (2010, May 10), Agreement will alter teacher evaluations. *New York Times,* retrieved from: www.nytimes.com/2010/05/11/nyregion/11teacher.html

129. Corcoran, S. P. (2010), *Can teachers be evaluated by their students' test scores? Should they be? The use of value-added measures of teacher effectiveness in policy and practice* (Providence, RI: Annenberg Institute for School Reform at Brown University).

130. Otterman, S. (2011, January 10), Judge rules that New York City can disclose names in teacher rankings; union plans to appeal. *New York Times,* retrieved from: www.nytimes.com/2011/01/11/education/11data.html

131. Otterman, S. (2011, September 15), City hands off part of teacher evaluation effort to the state. *New York Times,* retrieved from www.nytimes.com/2011/09/16/nyregion/new-york-hands-off-part-of-teacher-evaluation-effort.html

132. Hu, W. (2012, February 24), With teacher ratings set to be released, union opens campaign to discredit them. *New York Times,* retrieved from www.nytimes.com/2012/02/24/education/ratings-of-new-york-city-teachers-to-be-released-friday.html

133. Phillips, A. M. (2012, January 11), New York City charter school finds that a grade of 'C' means closing. *New York Times,* retrieved from www.nytimes.com/2012/01/12/education/new-york-city-plans-to-close-a-charter-school-for-mediocrity.html

134. Phillips, A. M. (2012, April 26), City decides to spare schools of second chances. *New York Times,* retrieved from www.nytimes.com/2012/04/27/nyregion/new-york-city-spares-bushwick-community-high-school-from-closing.html

135. Data source: NYC Department of Education website, schools.nyc.gov/NR/exeres/05289E74-2D81-4CC0-81F6-E1143E28F4C4,frameless.htm

136. Domanico, *State of New York City Public Schools 2002*.

137. Data source: NYC Department of Education website, schools.nyc.gov/Accountability/data/GraduationDropoutReports/default.htm

138. Ready, D., Hatch, T., Warner, M., Chu, E. (2013), *New York City schools: Following the learning trajectories of a cohort* (New York, NY: Education Funders Research Initiative), retrieved from edfundersresearch.albatrossdemos.com/research/new-york-city-schools-following-learning-trajectories-cohort/full

139. Ravitch, *Death and life of the great American school system*, p. 88.

140. Wilks, A. (2012, September), *Graduates, dropouts, discharges: Tracking four-year outcomes for the class of 2009*. Schools Brief (New York, NY: New York City Independent Budget Office), retrieved from www.ibo.nyc.ny.us/iboreports/gradrates2012.pdf

141. Ravitch, *Death and life of the great American school system*, p. 89.

142. Siskin, L. S. (2013), *College and career readiness in context* (New York, NY: Education Funders Research Initiative), retrieved from edfundersresearch.com/research/college-and-career-readiness-context/full

143. New York City Council Committee on Education (2002, March 19)

144. We have already discussed the modest improvements in state tests. James Kemple, from the Research Alliance for New York Schools, developed a statistical analysis to calculate the effects of Children First reforms on test scores. See Kemple, J. J. (2001), Children First and student outcomes 2003–2010, in O'Day et al., *Education reforms in New York City* (pp. 255–290).

145. New York City Council Committee on Education (2002, March 19)

Chapter 3: Toronto

1. Statistics Canada website, www.12.statcan.gc.ca

2. Ontario Ministry of Education website, www.edu.gov.on.ca

3. Anderson, S. E., & Ben Jaafar, S. (2003), *Policy trends in Ontario education 1990–2003* (Toronto, Canada: Ontario Institute for Studies in Education, University of Toronto).

4. Evidence of the demoralizing impact that the Common Sense Revolution had on secondary school teachers is provided in Hargreaves, A. (2003), *Teaching in the knowledge society* (New York, NY: Teachers College Press).

5. Gidney, R. D. (1999). From Hope to Harris: The reshaping of Ontario's schools (Toronto, Canada: University of Toronto Press).

6. Royal Commission on Learning (1994), *For the love of learning* (Toronto, Canada: Ontario Ministry of Education), retrieved from www.edu.gov.on.ca/eng/general/abcs/rcom/full/

7. O'Sullivan, B. (1999), Global change and educational reform in Ontario and Canada. *Canadian Journal of Education* 24(3), 311–325.

8. Anderson & Ben Jaafar, *Policy trends in Ontario education*.

9. EQAO website, www.eqao.com/

10. OCT website, www.oct.ca/about-the-college

11. See OCT website, www.oct.ca/public/professional-standards/standards-of-practice

12. Anderson & Ben Jaafar, *Policy trends in Ontario education.*

13. Anderson & Ben Jaafar, *Policy trends in Ontario education.*

14. Anderson & Ben Jaafar, *Policy trends in Ontario education.*

15. Education Equality Task Force (2002), *Investing in public education: Advancing the goal of continuous improvement in student learning and achievement* (Toronto, Canada: Ontario Ministry of Education).

16. DePalma, A. (1997, October 28), Teachers strike in Ontario, closing thousands of schools. *New York Times,* retrieved from www.nytimes.com/1997/10/28/world/teachers-strike-in-ontario-closing-thousands-of-schools.html

17. See People for Education website, www.peopleforeducation.ca/about-us/what-we-do/the-story-of-people-for-education/

18. Anderson & Ben Jaafar, *Policy trends in Ontario education.*

19. Royal Commission on Learning, *For the love of learning.*

20. Anderson & Ben Jaafar, *Policy trends in Ontario education.*

21. Anderson & Ben Jaafar, *Policy trends in Ontario education.*

22. Leithwood, K., Fullan, M., & Watson, N. (2003, January), *The schools we need: Recent education policy in Ontario with recommendations for moving forward* (Toronto, Canada: Ontario Institute for Studies in Education).

23. Leithwood, K., Fullan, M., & Watson, N. (2003, April), *The schools we need: A new blueprint for Ontario* (Toronto: Ontario Institute for Studies in Education), p. 2.

24. From *The Cure at Troy* (1991) by Seamus Heaney, retrieved from www.goodreads.com/author/quotes/29574.Seamus_Heaney

25. Fullan, M., Rolheiser, C., Mascall, B., & Edge, K. (2001), Accomplishing large-scale reform: A tri-level proposition (Toronto, Canada: Ontario Institute for Studies in Education, University of Toronto), retrieved from www.michaelfullan.ca/articles/. For a fuller account of the Ontario Strategy, see Glaze, A., Mattingley, R., & Andrews, R. (2013), *High school graduation* (Thousand Oaks, CA: Corwin Press).

26. Lorinc, J. (2004, October), Grade expectations. *Toronto Life,* p. 53, retrieved from www.michaelfullan.ca/articles/

27. See Council of Ministers of Education, Canada (2002), *School Achievement Indicators Program (SAIP): Report on Writing Assessment III* (Toronto, Canada: Council of Ministers of Education, Canada), retrieved from www.cmec.ca/Publications/Lists/Publications/Attachments/7/saip2002.en.pdf; Organization for Economic Cooperation and Development (OECD) (2003), *First Results from PISA 2003: Executive summary* (Paris, France: OECD), retrieved from www.oecd.org/education/school/programmeforinternationalstudentassessmentpisa/34002454.pdf

28. Organization for Economic Cooperation and Development (OECD) (2012), Ontario harnessing the skills of tomorrow, *in Strong performers and successful reformers in education: Lessons from PISA for Japan* (Chapter 5) (Paris, France: OECD).

29. Gallagher, M. J., Cameron, D. H., & Kokis, J. (2011, January), *The Ontario education strategy: The story of a comprehensive kindergarten to grade 12 large-scale reform,* paper presented to the International Congress for School Effectiveness and Improvement, Limassol, Cyprus

30. King, A., Warren, W. K., Boyer, J. C., & Chin, P. (2005), *Double cohort study: Phase 4 report, for the Ontario Ministry of Education* (Toronto, Canada: Ontario Ministry of Education).

31. At-Risk Working Group (2003), *A successful pathway for all students: Final report of the At-Risk Working Group* (Toronto, Canada: Ontario Ministry of Education).

32. Program Pathways for Students at Risk Work Group (2003), *Building pathways to success: Final report of the Program Pathways for Students at Risk Work Group* (Toronto, Canada: Ontario Ministry of Education).

33. King et al., *Double cohort study.*

34. Zegarac, G., & Franz. R. (2007, April), *Secondary school reform in Ontario and the role of research, evaluation and indicator data,* paper presented at the annual meeting of the American Educational Research Association, Chicago, IL.

35. Community Health Systems Resource Group, The Hospital for Sick Children (2005), *Early school leavers: Understanding the lived reality of student disengagement from secondary education* (Toronto, Canada: Ontario Ministry of Education).

36. See Ontario Ministry of Education (2013), *Specialist high skills major,* retrieved from www.edu.gov.on.ca/eng/studentsuccess/pathways/shsm/shsm_fact_sheet.pdf

37. Literacy and Numeracy Secretariat (2006), *Schools on the move: Lighthouse program* (Toronto, Canada: Ontario Ministry of Education, Literacy and Numeracy Secretariat).

38. Campbell, C., & Fullan, M. (2006), *Unlocking potential for learning: Effective district-wide strategies to raise student achievement in literacy and numeracy* (Toronto, Canada: Ontario Ministry of Education, Literacy and Numeracy Secretariat).

39. Olson, L. (2007, October 24), Ontario pins hopes on practices, not testing, to achieve. *Education Week, 27*(9), pp. 1, 12, 14.

40. Boyle, A. (2007), Compassionate intervention: Helping failing schools to turn around, *in* Blankstein, A. M., Cole, R. W., & Houston, P. D. (Eds.), *Engaging every learner* (pp. 147–172) (Thousand Oaks, CA: Corwin Press).

41. See Ontario Ministry of Education (2008), *Ontario focused intervention partnership (OFIP),* retrieved from www.edu.gov.on.ca/eng/literacynumeracy/ofip.html

42. Ungerleider, C. (2008), *Evaluation of the Ontario Ministry of Education's student success / learning to 18 strategy* (Ottawa, ON, Canada: Canadian Council on Learning), p. vi, retrieved from find.gov.on.ca/?searchType=simple&owner=edu&url=&collection=educationtcu&offset=0&lang=en&type=ANY&q=ungeleider+2007

43. Canadian Language and Literacy Research Network (2009), *The impact of the Literacy and Numeracy Secretariat: Changes in Ontario's education system* (London, ON, Canada: Canadian Language and Literacy Research Network), p. 11.

44. Fullan, M. (2006), *Change theory: A force for school improvement* (Victoria, Australia: Centre for Strategic Education), retrieved from www.michaelfullan.ca/articles/

45. Ontario Ministry of Education (2008), *Reach every student: Energizing Ontario education* (Toronto, Canada: Ontario Ministry of Education), retrieved from www.edu.gov.on.ca/eng/document/energize/energize.pdf

46. Pascal, C. E. (2009), *With our best future in mind: Implementing early learning in Ontario* (Toronto, Canada: Ontario Ministry of Education).

47. Early Learning Division, Ministry of Education (2012), *Modernizing child care in Ontario: Discussion Paper* (Toronto, Canada: Ontario Ministry of Education).

48. Ontario Ministry of Education (2013), *Ontario early years policy framework* (Toronto, Canada: Ontario Ministry of Education), retrieved from www.edu.gov. on.ca/childcare/OntarioEarlyYear.pdf

49. Ontario Ministry of Education (2008), *Finding common ground: Character development in Ontario schools, K–12* (Toronto, Canada: Ontario Ministry of Education), retrieved from www.edu.gov.on.ca/eng/document/reports/literacy/booklet2008.pdf

50. Ontario Ministry of Education (2009), *Reach every student through differentiated instruction: Grades 7 & 8* (Toronto, Canada: Ontario Ministry of Education), retrieved from www.edu.gov.on.ca/eng/teachers/buildingfutures/files/pdf/differentiated7and8.pdf

51. Lieberman, A. (2010), Teachers, learners, leaders. *Educational Leadership, 67;* retrieved from www.ascd.org/publications/educational-leadership/summer10/vol67/num09/Teachers,-Learners,-Leaders.aspx; Campbell, C., Lieberman, A., & Yashkina, A. (2013), *The teacher learning and leadership program: Research project* (Toronto, Canada: Ontario Ministry of Education and Ontario Teachers Federation).

52. Hine, E., & Maika, D. (2008, Fall), Why the teaching–learning critical pathway and why not? *Principal Connections, 12*(1), 16–19.

53. Literacy and Numeracy Secretariat (2010, September), *Collaborative teacher inquiry: New directions in professional practice*, Capacity Building Series No. 16 (Toronto, Canada: Ontario Ministry of Education, Literacy and Numeracy Secretariat).

54. Ontario Ministry of Education (2010), *Ontario leadership strategy: Strong and sustainable leadership for improved student achievement* (Toronto, Canada: Ontario Ministry of Education), retrieved from www.edu.gov.on.ca/eng/policyfunding/leadership/OLSPaper_September2010.pdf

55. Ontario Ministry of Education (2011), *Supporting the Ontario leadership strategy: Evaluation of the strategy September 2011* (Toronto, Canada: Ontario Ministry of Education), retrieved from www.edu.gov.on.ca/eng/policyfunding/memos/nov2011/EvaluationOLS.pdf

56. See Ontario Ministry of Education, retrieved from www.edu.gov.on.ca/eng/policyfunding/leadership/framework.html

57. Ontario Ministry of Education (2010), *School effectiveness framework K–12: A support for school improvement and student success* (Toronto, Canada: Ontario Ministry of Education), retrieved from www.edu.gov.on.ca/eng/literacynumeracy/Framework_english.pdf

58. Gallagher et al., *The Ontario education strategy.*

59. Literacy and Numeracy Secretariat (2009, August), *Critical literacy: A lens for learning,* Capacity Building Series No. 9 (Toronto, Canada: Ontario Ministry of Education, Literacy and Numeracy Secretariat).

60. For a description of all Student Success programs, see Ontario Ministry of Education (2011), *Student success,* retrieved from www.edu.gov.on.ca/ studentsuccess/

61. Office of Auditor General of Ontario (2011), Student success initiatives, *in Annual report* (Chapter 3, Section 3.13, pp. 269–287) (Toronto, Canada: Office of Auditor General of Ontario), retrieved from www.auditor.on.ca/en/reports_en/ en11/313en11.pdf

62. Office of Auditor General, Student success initiatives.

63. Ontario Ministry of Education (2009), *Equity and inclusive education in Ontario schools: Guidelines for policy development and implementation* (Toronto, Canada: Ontario Ministry of Education).

64. Office of Auditor General, Student success initiatives, p. 270.

65. Office of Auditor General, Student success initiatives, p. 278.

66. Ontario Education Research Symposium (2009), *Closing gaps in student achievement: Summary Report* (Toronto, Canada: Ontario Ministry of Education), retrieved from www.edu.gov.on.ca/eng/research/2009SummaryReport.pdf

67. Working Table on Special Education (2006), *Special education transformation: Report of the Working Table on Special Education* (Toronto, Canada: Ontario Ministry of Education), retrieved from www.edu.gov.on.ca/eng/document/reports/ speced/transformation/transformation.pdf

68. Expert Panel on Literacy and Numeracy Instruction for Students with Special Educational Needs (2005), *Education for all: Report of Expert Panel on Literacy and Numeracy Instruction for Students with Special Educational Needs K–6* (Toronto, Canada: Ontario Ministry of Education), retrieved from www.edu.gov.on.ca/ eng/document/reports/speced/panel/speced.pdf

69. Hargreaves, A., & Braun, H. (2012), *Leading for all: The CODE special education project* (Toronto, Canada: Council of Ontario Directors of Education), retrieved from www.ontariodirectors.ca/downloads/Essential_FullReport_Final.pdf

70. Office of Auditor General of Ontario (2008), Special education, *in Annual report* (Chapter 3, Section 3.14, pp. 364–386) (Toronto, Canada: Office of Auditor General of Ontario), p. 366.

71. Ontario Ministry of Education (2011), *Learning for all: A guide to effective assessment and instruction for all students kindergarten to Grade 12* (Toronto, Canada: Ontario Ministry of Education), retrieved from www.edu.gov.on.ca/eng/general /elemsec/speced/LearningforAll2011.pdf

72. Coelho, E. (2007), *How long does it take? Lessons from EQAO data on English language learners in Ontario schools* (Toronto, Canada: Ontario Literacy and Numeracy Secretariat), retrieved from www.edu.gov.on.ca/eng/literacynumeracy/ inspire/equity/ell_july30.html

73. Ontario Ministry of Education (2005), *Many roots many voices: Supporting English language learners in every classroom* (Toronto, Canada: Ontario Ministry of Education), retrieved from www.edu.gov.on.ca/eng/document/manyroots/manyroots.pdf

74. Ontario Ministry of Education (2007), *English language learners: Policies and procedures for Ontario elementary and secondary schools, K–12* (Toronto, Canada: Ontario Ministry of Education), retrieved from www.edu.gov.on.ca/eng/document/esleldprograms/esleldprograms.pdf

75. See Ontario Ministry of Education (2012), *The Ontario curriculum: Secondary English as a second language and English literacy development* (Toronto, Canada: Ontario Ministry of Education), retrieved from www.edu.gov.on.ca/eng/curriculum/secondary/esl.html

76. Aboriginal Education Office (2007), *Ontario First Nation, Métis and Inuit education policy framework* (Toronto, Canada: Ontario Ministry of Education), retrieved from www.edu.gov.on.ca/eng/aboriginal/fnmiframework.pdf

77. Aboriginal Education Office (2007), *Aboriginal education in Ontario: New resources and opportunities for parents, educators and students* (Toronto, Canada: Ontario Ministry of Education), retrieved from www.edu.gov.on.ca/eng/aboriginal/new_resources.pdf

78. Cherubini, L., Hodson, J., Manley-Casimir, M., & Muir, C. (2010), Closing the gap at the peril of widening the void: Implications of the Ontario Ministry of Education's policy for Aboriginal education. *Canadian Journal of Education, 33*(2), 329–355.

79. Aboriginal Education Office (2007), *Building bridges to success for First Nation, Métis and Inuit students* (Toronto, Canada: Ontario Ministry of Education), retrieved from www.edu.gov.on.ca/eng/Aboriginal/buildBridges.pdf

80. Office of Auditor General of Ontario (2012), Education of Aboriginal students, *in Annual report* (Chapter 3, Section 3.05, pp. 129–148) (Toronto, Canada: Office of Auditor General of Ontario), p. 130.

81. Office of Auditor General, Education of Aboriginal students, p. 139.

82. Office of Auditor General, Education of Aboriginal students, pp. 139–140.

83. Bodkin, B., & OISE Research Team (2009), *The road ahead: Boys' literacy teacher inquiry project 2005–2008* (Toronto, Canada: Ontario Ministry of Education), retrieved from www.edu.gov.on.ca/eng/curriculum/RoadAhead2009.pdf

84. Literacy and Numeracy Secretariat (2010), *OFIP 1/2, 2009–2010: Lessons Learned* (Toronto, Canada: Ontario Ministry of Education), retrieved from www.edu.gov.on.ca/eng/literacynumeracy/research/ofip12report.pdf

85. People for Education (2012), *Making connections beyond school walls: Annual report on Ontario's publically funded schools* (Toronto, Canada: People for Education), retrieved from www.peopleforeducation.ca/wp-content/uploads/2012/05/Annual-Report-2012-web.pdf

86. Fullan, M. (2013), *Great to excellent: Launching the next stage of Ontario's education agenda* (Toronto, Canada: Ontario Ministry of Education).

87. Kerr, L. (2006), *Between caring and counting: Teachers take on education reform* (Toronto, Canada: University of Toronto Press).

88. Kerr, *Between caring and counting.*

89. Rushowy, K. (2008, October 6), Rudderless school board "on edge." *Toronto Star,* retrieved from www.thestar.com/life/parent/2008/10/06/rudderless_school_board_on_edge.html

90. Rushowy, Rudderless school board.

91. Brown, L. (2013, January 11), Chris Spence: charismatic "agent of change" falls hard. *Toronto Star,* retrieved from www.thestar.com/news/gta/2013/01/11/chris_spence_charismatic_agent_of_change_falls_hard.html

92. Brown, Chris Spence.

93. Zheng, S. (2013), *The effectiveness of the Toronto District School Board's teacher professional learning in the 2012–2013 blended professional learning community* (Toronto, Canada: TDSB).

94. The capacity-building series of publications is available at www.edu.gov.on.ca/eng/literacynumeracy/inspire/research/capacityBuilding.html

95. For TDSB Equity Foundation Statement, see Toronto District School Board (1999), Policy P.037 CUR (Toronto, Canada: TDSB), retrieved from www.tdsb.on.ca/Portals/0/HighSchool/docs/200.pdf; for Ontario Equity and Inclusive Education Strategy, see Ontario Ministry of Education (2013), *Greater equity means greater student success* (Toronto, Canada: Ontario Ministry of Education), retrieved from www.edu.gov.on.ca/eng/policyfunding/equity.html

96. For details of TDSB census publications and census portraits, see www.tdsb.on.ca/AboutUs/Research/ParentandStudentCensus/CensusPublications

97. For details of Model Schools for Inner Cities, see www.tdsb.on.ca/Community/ModelSchoolsforInnerCities.aspx

Chapter 4: London

1. Data source: Office for National Statistics, retrieved from www.ons.gov.uk/ons/rel/regional-trends/region-and-country-profiles/region-and-country-profiles—key-statistics-and-profiles—october-2013/key-statistics-and-profiles—london—october-2013.html

2. In the United Kingdom the word "college" applies to many different education institutions. Some schools use the word "college" in their title. So does the National College for School Leadership.

3. Agenda benders [Editorial] (1995, June 19), *Times Higher Education Supplement,* retrieved from www.timeshighereducation.co.uk/news/agenda-benders/98739.article

4. National Commission on Education (Great Britain) (1996), *Success against the odds: Effective schools in disadvantaged areas* (London, England: Routledge).

5. Earl, L. M. (2000), *Watching and learning: OISE/UT evaluation of the implementation of the national literacy and numeracy strategies* (Toronto, Canada: Ontario Institute for Studies in Education, University of Toronto).

6. Hatcher, R., & Leblond, D. (2001, June), *Education Action Zones and zones d'education prioritaires*, paper presented at conference on *Travelling Policy/Local Spaces: Globalization, Identities and Education Policy in Europe*, Keele University, Keele, Staffordshire, UK.

7. Gewirtz, S., Dickson, M., & Power, S. (2007), Unravelling a "spun" policy: A case study of the constitutive role of "spin" in the education process, *in* Lingard, B., & Ozga, J. (Eds.), *Routledge Falmer Reader in Education Policy and Politics* (pp. 178–197) (London, England: Routledge).

8. Her Majesty's Inspectors of Schools (HMI) (2003), *Education Action Zones: Tackling difficult issues in round 2 zones* (London, England: Office for Standards in Education).

9. Machin, S., McNally, S., & Meghir, C. (2007), *Resources and standards in urban schools* (London, England: Centre for the Economics of Education, London School of Economics); Her Majesty's Inspectors of Schools (HMI) (2005), *Excellence in cities* (London, England: Office for Standards in Education).

10. House of Commons Education and Skills Committee (May 2003), *Secondary education: Diversity of provision*, Report (London, England: The Stationery Office).

11. Brighouse, T. (2007), The London challenge–a personal view, *in* Brighouse, T., & Fullick, L. (Eds.), *Education in a global city: Essays from London* (pp. 71–94) (London, England: Institute of Education), p. 77.

12. Hargreaves, A., et al. (2011), *Performance beyond expectations* (Nottingham, England: National College for School Leadership), retrieved from www.national-college.org.uk/docinfo?id=151888&filename=performance-beyond-expectations-full-report.pdf

13. Hackett, G. (1998, October 9), Managers blamed for poor standards. *Times Educational Supplement*, retrieved from www.tes.co.uk/article.aspx?storycode=79239

14. Mansell, W. (2000, June 23), Radicals transform Tower Hamlets. *Times Educational Supplement*, retrieved from www.tes.co.uk/article.aspx?storycode=336187

15. Audit Commission (2000, November), *Hackney LBC: Corporate governance inspection* (London, England: Audit Commission).

16. For a detailed evaluation of how The Learning Trust improved education in Hackney, see Boyle, A., & Humphreys, S. (2012), *A revolution in a decade: Ten out of ten* (London, England: Leannta).

17. Bubb, S., & Earley, P. (2007), The school workforce in London, *in* Brighouse & Fullick, *Education in a global city* (London, England: Institute of Education) (pp. 147–168).

18. See Chartered London Teacher website, www.clt.ac.uk/

19. Brighouse, The London challenge, p. 85.

20. Office for Standards in Education (Ofsted) (2010), *London Challenge* (London, England: Office for Standards in Education).

21. Ofsted, *London Challenge*, p. 5.

22. See Families of Schools section on the UK government website, www.education.gov.uk/publications/standard/publicationDetail/Page1/DFE-00047-2011

23. Brighouse, The London Challenge. p. 86.

24. Ofsted, *London Challenge*, p. 6.

25. Ofsted, *London Challenge*, p. 4.

26. For more information about the research methodologies, see Hargreaves et al., *Performance beyond expectations.*

27. You may watch a YouTube clip of Sir Alasdair Macdonald talking about the challenge of closing achievement gaps in high-poverty schools during times of austerity at www.youtube.com/watch?v=4i_FCLIt5-M

28. Boyle & Humphreys, *A revolution in a decade.*

29. Office for Standards in Education (Ofsted) (1999), *Lessons learned from special measures* (London, England: Office for Standards in Education).

30. See Fullan, M. (2010), *All systems go* (Thousand Oaks, CA: Corwin Press).

31. Boyle & Humphreys, *A revolution in a decade,* p. 36.

32. Boyle & Humphreys, *A Revolution in a decade,* p. 67.

33. Boyle & Humphreys, *A revolution in a decade,* p. 120.

34. Boyle & Humphreys, *A revolution in a decade,* p. 111.

Chapter 5: Lessons Learned

1. Retrieved from www.nytimes.com/2013/07/14/opinion/sunday/the-trouble-with-testing-mania.html?_r=0

2. Fullan, M. & Langworthy, M. (2014), *A rich seam: How new pedagogies find deep learning* (London, England: Pearson).

Index

About the Authors

Michael Fullan, Order of Canada, is professor emeritus of the Ontario Institute for Studies in Education at the University of Toronto, and served as special adviser on education to the Premier of Ontario, Dalton McGuinty. He consults widely on system reform in countries around the world and conducts workshops on leadership for change. Professor Fullan has written a number of award-winning books that have been published in many languages. His latest books are *Change Leader, Putting the FACES on Data* (with Lyn Sharratt), *Stratosphere: Integrating Technology, Pedagogy, and Change Knowledge; Professional Capital* (with Andy Hargreaves), and *The Principal.* His website is www.michaelfullan.ca.

Alan Boyle is director of Leannta Education Associates; he designs professional learning for education leaders in the United Kingdom and abroad. Over the last 12 years he has maintained links and annual exchange visits between school districts in England and Ontario. Between 2006 and 2008 he worked as a consultant to help establish Quality Review in NYC. As a researcher, he contributed to the Performance Beyond Expectations project and investigated high-performing organizations in business, education, and sport from 2007–2010. During 2011–2012 he carried out a long-term review of the work of The Learning Trust that was published as *A Revolution in a Decade: Ten out of Ten.*

Alan started his career as a teacher and spent 20 years in urban classrooms across England teaching students mainly from low-income families. He moved into district administration, working for two inner-city local authorities including seven years as chief inspector in a London borough. He has written science textbooks, many articles in journals and newspapers, and the chapter "Compassionate Intervention" in *Engaging Every Learner.* He was invited to present the honors lecture at the National Science Teachers Association annual conference in Houston and from time to time presents papers or workshops at AERA and Learning Forward. He enjoys climbing mountains.